FIRST STEPS
IN
THE BIBLE

FIRST STEPS
IN
THE BIBLE

RUTH GRAHAM DIENERT

WORD BOOKS
PUBLISHER
WACO, TEXAS
76703

Title page and illustrations
used in chapters 22, 27, 45, 51, 57, 70, 74, 83, and 88
from the private collection of Ronald E. Garman
and are used with permission.
Photograph for chapter 39 by Marilee Zdenek.
Photograph for chapter 80 by Michael A. Riley.
Photograph for chapter 81 by Steven Wilson.
All other photographs are courtesy of Russ Busby.

ISBN 0-8499-2972-5
Library of Congress catalog card number: 79-63939
Printed in the United States of America

First printing: October 1980
First paperback printing: August 1983
Second paperback printing: June 1984

Acknowledgments

No book is one person's effort. It takes many people who contribute time, encouragement and advice.

I would like to express gratitude to Mr. Charles Foster who first published *First Steps for Little Feet Along Gospel Paths* in the early 1800s. It has been a classic children's Bible story book; I have only tried to update it for our modern times.

I would like to say thank you to my mother, Ruth Graham, for suggesting I begin this project; to Julie Eisenhower for her enthusiastic encouragement; to Bonnie Lembright and Linda Boice for their advice and counsel; to Barbara Hershey, who helped manage my household so that I could write; to Louise Tabasso, Patty Young, and Roseann Sansone, who typed and proofread by the hour; to my children, Noelle, Graham, and Windsor, for whom I started this project; and to my husband, Ted, and his father, Fred Dienert, who undertook the business end of it.

Especially, I am grateful to Russ Busby for the artistic and sensitive photographs he contributed to this book. They are a valuable contribution.

And lastly, I would like to thank Word Books, Publisher, who believed in this project, and my editor, Pat Wienandt, and artist-designer, Ronald Garman, who helped make it a reality.

Introduction

Three Generations

It was a memorable day when I received my own copy of *First Steps for Little Feet Along Gospel Paths* by Charles Foster. I don't recall what the occasion was, probably the achievement of memorizing a certain portion of Scripture. But whatever the reason, I cherished this little book. I could not read yet, but I remember gently leafing through the book, looking at the pictures and anticipating the day when I could read it for myself.

I was not the first child in my family to receive this book. Many years before, when my grandparents, then medical missionaries to China, searched for a book from which to guide their children to an early understanding of Biblical truths, they chose *First Steps for Little Feet Along Gospel Paths*. They saw that this book built precept upon precept in teaching little ones the great principles and facts of the Christian faith. So they read and reread this book to their children.

In turn, my mother, so often alone trying to raise five children, turned to this book for our preschool training. She had discovered that it had a delightful way of presenting the basic doctrines of faith so that a child could grasp them, understand them and take them as his or her own.

She not only read it to us and quizzed us with the questions that followed each chapter but made us see that this was a cherished book to be loved. It gave us an early appreciation for the Bible and told us of the historical examples we could follow as we were growing up, for example, Daniel. We learned early that the Bible was an exciting and practical book to be relied upon in every situation.

As I grew up, it stayed on my bookshelf along with all the other books that changed as I changed interest. This book remained, along with my Bible. When I was small, I read it to my dolls; then, as I grew, it was left alone except when I'd occasionally pull it down to see my childlike attempt to write my name in the front. When I married, it was packed along with my other books and moved to my new home. It sat on the bookshelf for several years, still cherished.

Then I had two children very close together, with a third to come later. When my husband and I thought that they had reached an age where they could respond to a family prayer time, we proceeded with gusto. I went to the store and bought all the new Bible story books: books on how to have an exciting family devotion; idea books; everything I thought would help us to get started. For the first few days, things went fairly well, but eventually the plan fizzled. So I went back to the store looking for a gimmick. I talked to friends for ideas and sympathy.

Finally, I remembered *First Steps for Little Feet Along Gospel Paths* on my shelf. My children got great delight in seeing my name scrawled in pencil in the front and they were excited about a book their Mommy read when she was little and even their Tai Tai (what they call my Mother; pronounced Teddy, meaning "old lady" in Chinese) read when she was a little girl in China.

So we began. The children enjoyed it. The chapters were short, and since they knew they would have questions asked of them, they paid close attention. The family devotion time took us a total of about ten to fifteen minutes. My three-and-a-half-year-old daughter thought it was great and did very well. And even though my two-year-old son couldn't answer the questions too accurately, he was getting the gist of it.

Updating

As we progressed through the book it became increasingly clear that the book needed updating. The language of the 1800s sounded strange in the twentieth century. So I began to edit words and phrases as I went along. The concept of the book was still excellent—a classic; it just needed modernizing.

On a visit to my parents' home in North Carolina one Easter, I told my mother that the book needed to be rewritten and suggested that she do it. But she turned around and said that she thought I should do it. As I began to edit and rewrite and add some original material I became aware of the value of this book as a tool in teaching young children. Mr. Foster's concept of building upon a foundation, precept upon precept, was strong. And when I would look up in Scripture to double-check a fact, I was impressed with the accuracy of the book. It was an exciting project for me.

Revisions

Above all, I did not want to tamper with Mr. Foster's concept. I did edit words and phrases that were outdated, and I revised some material. I wrote some original chapters that I thought would contribute to the overall development of the book. Some chapters I eliminated when I thought they were repetitive.

However, I have added many new

and, I believe, helpful ideas throughout the book. First, it is a better size for reading to children—more easily visible as they sit beside you when you are reading. The seventy-eight illustrations, fifty-two in full color, will capture a child's imagination. Also, throughout the book there are "parental notes" to help you, as parents, to guide your children into an understanding of the principles set forth.

A Unique Book

As you go through this book with your child you will notice that it is far from being a surface Bible story book. It begins with God's act of Creation, His maintaining and caring for that Creation. Then I have introduced the idea that we have a responsibility to take care of His creation and not destroy what God has given us to enjoy. I introduce the basic doctrines, through Bible stories, of the reality of Satan and his demons, obedience to God, original sin, Christ's atoning death, eternal life and so forth. Where I have thought it to be helpful or appropriate in calling attention to these doctrines, I have made notes concerning them.

Children understand these principles in an amazing way and readily accept them. It is easy for us, as adults, to make these things too complicated. Children want to believe and have such open hearts towards the things of God. It is an exciting experience to see your child respond to the love of God when he or she has been told of it simply and sweetly.

All Scriptural quotations are from the New International Version so that the child will become familiar with actual Scripture and its wording. Each chapter has a reference so that you can go back to the Bible and read it or check on something for yourself, as I did when I was revising the book. Every seventh chapter has an appropriate memory verse suggestion. I feel it is important for a child to begin memorizing verses early and to make this a lifelong habit. One verse a week is a good goal at the start.

The photographs are included to catch a child's imagination and keep his attention. Some are photographs of great art masterpieces, to enlarge a child's world; some are of actual locations, such as Bethlehem, that underscore the historicity of the Bible, its people, and events; and some show the lifestyle of Biblical times to give the child an idea of how people lived and still do live in another part of the world. With each story, discuss the picture that is relevant. Ask questions about the picture, such as: What do you think is happening? How do you think these people felt? What would you have done? Try to get the child involved in the story.

Devotions for the Family

When I was growing up, my family had family prayers right after breakfast. That is ideal—to start the day off with prayer together. My husband and I have found that a good time for our family is right after dinner. Things don't seem quite so rushed, and we are all together and refreshed by a good meal. It is important to keep things short—only ten to fifteen minutes. My mother always said about anything in life, "Know when to quit." Try to be regular and consistent.

How to Start

Read a chapter of *First Steps in the Bible,* ask the questions, and then have a short prayer. If you have very young children, the questions might be a bit difficult and you may want to rephrase them so that the answer is in the question. For instance, in chapter one, one of the first questions is: What hangs in my mother's kitchen?" Instead, you might ask, "Does a birdcage hang in my mother's kitchen?"

Or you could make it a multiple choice: "What hangs in my mother's kitchen—a birdcage, a monkey, or a vine?" For the older child, I have added a more difficult "thought" question at the end of most chapters.

When it comes to the prayer time, on some occasions our children like to have short sentence prayers so that each one in turn can pray out loud. Remember to teach your children to praise and thank the Lord first. Always be specific in your requests as well as in your praise. Perhaps you could begin a family prayer list which would include friends, teachers, school work, pastor, missionaries, the President and world leaders, and others. And when you see answers, be sure to point them out to your children and talk about how good God is to answer our prayers. We like to kneel for prayer.

Something I love to do with my children is sing. Unfortunately, I inherited my father's monotone, but the children don't care. This is a marvelous way for them to learn the great hymns of the church. In fact, instead of singing lullabies to my babies, I always sang hymns like "Amazing Grace," "The Old Rugged Cross," "Oh For A Thousand Tongues," and so forth. My grandparents and parents gave me a valuable legacy by teaching me the hymns. Since our small community church had no Sunday evening service, we would round up friends, gather in the living room, and sing hymns. These "hymn sings" were always fun. Also, if we traveled by car we would sing together hymns and choruses. It was marvelous family fun but we learned hymns that we've treasured all our lives.

Keep things happy. Expect to have squirming and wiggling and a few interruptions when you are reading to little ones. It is surprising how much they absorb even while squirming. Don't make it a pressured competitive situation. If a child cannot answer a question or has not listened very well, don't fuss; they will probably get it the next time around. With ninety-one chapters you have lots of variety and can use this little book over and over again!

Family Togetherness Time

I love to read to my children! And it's a wonderful way to spend concentrated time with them. By reading together we can travel to faraway places, meet interesting people, silly characters and have outlandish adventures. Reading can also spark marvelous conversations with your children. Learn to listen to them. Try to make your reading exciting by voice inflection. (My mother had such a wonderful Scottish brogue and my grandmother could imitate all the Southern accents.) Use *First Steps in the Bible* as a catalyst for family time; gather together for a time of fun and spiritual training. You will be surprised what this will lead to as far as family growth and closeness is concerned. And God will bless your efforts. Ideally, it's nice to have the father lead family prayers, but if he is away, as my husband is so much of the time, the mother can fill in.

A Book to Enjoy

But *First Steps in the Bible* does not have to be limited to family devotions. Place it where it can be easily reached for little ones to look at on their own, or for older ones to read to themselves. Let them use it as a reference book for Sunday School lessons. It is a book to be used and enjoyed by the whole family. While your aim as parents may be to use it for spiritual development in your children, they don't have to be aware of that!

My mother always says, "The best way to get a child to eat is to have him see his parents enjoying their food." So it is with spiritual training!

And so, you have in your hands a

unique book that has been tested by time and that has contributed to the nurturing of three generations. It is a classic. The revisions have enhanced *First Steps* by adding beautiful photographs that will expand a child's world through color, art, geography and culture; by adding memory verse guidelines to help establish a lifelong habit; by adding the Bible reference for each chapter so that you can refer back to Scripture; and by adding many helpful parental notes to guide you.

It is my prayer that you enjoy this book together with your little ones and that God will use it to draw your family not only closer to each other but closer to Him.

Bunny Dienert
Argyle, Texas

CHAPTER 1

Genesis 1:3–5; 14–19; 26–27

MEMORY VERSE—Genesis 1:1 In the beginning God created the heavens and the earth.

Do you know what is hanging in my mother's kitchen? A birdcage. And inside the birdcage sits a bright yellow bird called a canary that sings all day long at the top of his lungs. His name is "Cheerful." Mother named him that because his singing, even on cloudy days, sounds so cheerful.

The birdcage is very shiny and shaped like a Japanese house. I remember when she bought it at the store. Some man made that cage so he could sell it for money. But he didn't make Mother's little bird, "Cheerful."

Men can make cages, chairs, cars, houses, and many, many other things, but men can't make things that are alive. Only God can do that.

God lives in heaven. We cannot see Him, but He sees us all the time, even during the night!

At night it is dark. We get ready for bed and get tucked into bed to sleep. Even "Cheerful" fluffs up his feathers and goes to sleep when the sun goes down.

And when the sun goes down, pretty soon we see the moon shining and the stars twinkling up in the sky. But, in the morning, when the sun comes up, we can't see the stars and moon any more.

God made the sun and the moon and the stars up in the sky to be lights for us. Without them it would be very, very dark, and we couldn't see anything.

And did you know God made you, too? You are very special to Him; He loves you and cares all about you.

Now I'm going to ask you some questions about what I just read to you. Let's see if you remember.

QUESTIONS—CHAPTER 1

1. *What hangs in my mother's kitchen?*
2. *What is in the cage? Do you remember his name?*
3. *Who made the cage?*
4. *Who made "Cheerful"?*
5. *Who makes things that are alive?*
6. *Where does God live?*
7. *Can He see us all the time?*
8. *Who made the sun, moon, and stars and put them in the sky?*
9. *What would it be like without the sun and moon?*
10. *Who else did God make?*
11. *Does He love you very much?*

Look at these beautiful birds. God made them that way. Did you know that God made you, too? You are very special and beautiful to Him.

CHAPTER 2

There are many other things we see up in the sky. On a pretty spring day, I love to lie down in the grass and watch the clouds float along in the sky. God made those clouds.

Sometimes they bring rain and, if you live up north as I do, the clouds bring snow in the wintertime. It's fun to get up in the morning and discover that during the night snow has covered the ground. We bundle up warmly in coat, hat, boots, and gloves to go outside to play. And we make a special kind of maple candy that we only make when it snows.

God made the rain and snow that comes down from the clouds.

After the snow melts in springtime, I like to run out to where I know there are some flowers planted. And I look to see if they are beginning to come up. And do you know what? They are coming up. Even under all that snow and cold weather, they know when to begin to grow.

God tells them when.

I love springtime when the birds begin to sing again, the grass gets green, and the leaves come back on the trees. And I like to watch the big fat robins hopping about on the lawn getting worms.

QUESTIONS—CHAPTER 2

1. *What else do we see up in the sky besides the sun, moon, and stars?*
2. *What do clouds bring?*
3. *After the snow melts what comes up from the ground?*
4. *Who tells them to come up?*

God made the rain and snow that come down from the clouds. The earth drinks the rain and helps seeds to grow into lovely flowers like these.

CHAPTER 3

One day when I was walking outside, I saw in a bush a bundle of dry grass and little sticks all twisted together. It was a bird's nest. And a bird was sitting in it. The bird had a little beak, black shiny eyes, and a red breast. It was a robin.

I watched for a long time and it flew away. When it did I saw three baby birds in the nest. Soon the mother robin came back, and in her beak was a worm. She fed it to the baby birds. Baby birds love worms, just as girls and boys love peanut butter and jelly.

Sometimes in summer you may see a very small bird, so small that you wonder if it really is a bird—it's about the size of your little finger. And if you listen very carefully, you can hear a humming noise. That is a hummingbird.

One morning, I looked out my window and sitting very still on a tree limb, I saw a big owl. Every so often he would turn his head and hoot. Owls usually sleep in the daytime and wake up at night. The owl was very big and held onto the limb with sharp claws. He uses those claws to pick up his food and fly away.

Ducks and geese are birds, too. Maybe they fly over your house in the spring and fall as they do over mine. God made them, too.

If your mother and father ever took you to the zoo and visited the big birdhouse there—it's called an aviary—you saw all the many different kinds of birds God made. Some have beautiful colors, some are funny looking; some are big, some small. But God made them all.

God made all the birds and taught them how to build nests and find food.

QUESTIONS—CHAPTER 3

1. *What did I see in the bush?*
2. *What was in the nest when the mama bird flew away?*
3. *When she came back what did she have in her mouth?*
4. *What did she do with the worm?*
5. *Who made all the birds and taught them how to build nests and find food?*

This hummingbird is very small, no bigger than your little finger. Imagine how small its babies are! God makes them all and loves them, no matter how small.

CHAPTER 4

God made all the animals, too. There are all kinds of animals, as there are all kinds of birds. Some animals are wild and live out in the woods or jungle, like wolves and bears and tigers. Other animals are tame like sheep and cows.

If you've ever been to the zoo, you've seen lots of different kinds of animals. The wild animals are usually in a cage so they can't hurt us or people hurt them. The tame animals are put in a special area so we can pet them.

Not far from my house there is a sheep farm. In the spring it's fun to go see all the woolly baby lambs.

Wool grows on the sheep's back. When it's time, men take big scissors, called shears, and cut the wool off the sheep's back. Then it is cleaned, made into yarn or thread and people make clothes out of it. The warm sweater or thick coat you have for winter is probably made out of wool that grew on a sheep's back.

Tigers and lions are very fierce and could hurt us, but they live in countries very far from here. We can go see them in the zoo, where we are protected from them, or we can look at pretty pictures of them. They are very beautiful and strong animals. God made them that way.

QUESTIONS—CHAPTER 4

1. *Who made the animals?*
2. *What grows on a sheep's back?*
3. *What is made out of the wool?*
4. *Are tigers and bears fierce?*
5. *Who made them that way?*

Doesn't this lion look big and strong? God made him that way. God made all the animals, some of them big and fierce, some of them small and tame. He loves them all.

CHAPTER 5

In my doctor's office there is a big glass tank full of water. It's called an aquarium because fish live there. Fish also live in streams and rivers, oceans and lakes, or maybe a pond in your back yard.

Fish don't have feet or legs like animals, or wings like birds; instead God gave them fins so they could swim in the water. And they have a special way of breathing—through gills—so they can stay in the water all the time.

There are many kinds of fish. Some are very small and some have beautiful colors. Some are very big and some are funny looking. Some fish we never see because they live at the bottom of the ocean.

God made all the fish and everything in the oceans. He made the beautiful goldfish and He also made the huge whale. He takes care of them and has given them all that they need to live in the water.

QUESTIONS—CHAPTER 5

1. *Who made the fish?*
2. *Do they have wings and feet?*
3. *What do they have instead?*
4. *Where did God make the fish live?*
5. *Did God give them all they need to live in the water?*

God made all the fish and everything in the oceans. He takes care of them and gives them all they need to live in the water.

CHAPTER 6

One day I went into the country to buy honey from a man who had lots of bees. The bees lived in several houses he had made for them called hives. And one hive had a glass wall so that if I were very careful not to get stung I could see the bees making honey in the hive.

During the summer days, the bee goes out of its house to find and collect nectar from the flowers. Nectar is the sweet sugary liquid in flowers that bees use to make honey. The bee keeps on going from flower to flower until it has collected enough nectar to fill its honey stomach. He keeps on going back and forth to his hive with this nectar until he and the other bees have filled the hive. That is why in the summertime there are usually bees buzzing around the pretty flowers.

When the hive is full of honey, made by the bees from nectar, men come and get the honey to take home or to sell it. It is very good to eat; it tastes very sweet.

Also in the summertime, we see beautiful butterflies flying from flower to flower. They are very pretty. They have large wings that are usually brightly colored. Some have red wings or yellow wings or blue.

Bees and butterflies are insects. There are many kinds of insects. Some are useful like the bee; some are pretty like the butterfly, and some are aggravating like the fly. There is one little insect that flies around at night and makes a bright light wherever it goes, just as if it were carrying a little lamp with it. It is called a firefly.

God made all the insects. God made all the living things in this world and takes care of them.

QUESTIONS—CHAPTER 6

1. *What did I buy from the man in the country?*
2. *Who made the honey?*
3. *What is the name of the little house the bees live in?*
4. *What is the insect that looks as if it were carrying a little lamp?*
5. *Who made all the insects and living things?*

Thought Question, chapters 1–6: The Bible says that you are made in God's image. When you create something—a picture, a cake, a model, are you reflecting God's image in you? That's pretty neat, isn't it? What do you think God is telling us through His creation? What does the story of the Creation tell us about God?

Parental Note: The study of bees, their work, organization and cooperation is fascinating. You may want to pull out an encyclopedia and read to your children about them, pointing out how wonderfully God made everything. He saw to each detail.

God makes all the insects, like bees and butterflies and flies. Did you know that this butterfly was once a little caterpillar?

CHAPTER 7

Sometimes, especially in the spring or fall, when you are driving in the car with your mother or father, you may see a squirrel or bird that has been hit by a car and killed. It makes me sad when I see it.

Maybe you might say to your Mother, "God will make it all better," or you might ask, "Wasn't God taking care of that bird or squirrel?"

The answer to that starts a long time ago. When God made the world and all the birds, animals, and fish, He looked around at all He had made and said something was missing. So He decided to make a man. And he did. But when God saw the man He said that Adam, the man, should not be all by himself, so He made a woman, called Eve.

God was very happy to have made Adam and Eve. He put them in a beautiful garden, called Eden, that was full of wonderful plants and animals and birds. Everything was perfect. No one cried or was sick or died. All the animals loved the other animals and birds. No one hurt anyone else. God gave Adam and Eve everything they needed and told them to enjoy everything. But He told them that there was one tree in the garden from which they could not eat the fruit. He told them that

they must obey Him.

Everything was happy until one day when Eve began to talk with a very beautiful creature named Satan. He made her question what God had said to her about the fruit tree. Soon Satan made Eve think that it wasn't as important to obey God as she had thought, and she ate some of the fruit from that tree. She gave some to Adam, too.

All of a sudden they realized that they had been very wrong to listen to Satan and disobey God. When they heard God coming in the Garden, they hid from Him.

God was very sad because He knew what Adam and Eve had done. They had disobeyed Him—that is called a sin. God knew He would have to punish them.

When God saw Adam and Eve, He told them what the punishment for their sin was. Part of the punishment was death.

Ever since Adam and Eve sinned by disobeying God, people, animals, birds and fish have died.

But God has provided a wonderful way for us to live forever. He sent His Son Jesus to take the punishment for us so that when we die we can go to heaven and live forever. All we have to do is ask His Son, Jesus, into our hearts to wash away our sins, and He does! Isn't that exciting?

QUESTIONS—CHAPTER 7

1. *What was missing when God looked at all He had made?*
2. *What did God make?*
3. *What was the man's name?*
4. *What was the woman's name?*
5. *What was the name of the Garden?*
6. *Was the Garden of Eden perfect?*
7. *What did God tell Adam and Eve not to do?*
8. *What was the name of the beautiful creature Eve began to talk to?*
9. *Who did Satan make Eve doubt?*
10. *What did Eve do?*
11. *What did she then realize?*
12. *Why did Adam and Eve hide from God?*
13. *Was God sad?*
14. *What was the punishment?*

Thought Question: When Adam and Eve sinned, why did that affect everyone else ever to be born?

Parental Note: This chapter contains many concepts: the reality of Satan and his activity of trying to get us to disobey God; penalty for disobeying God; the atoning death of Christ; eternal life; and original sin. Don't let so much frighten you. Children accept these things so easily and do not question them. Do not make it complicated; just present it as it is.

CHAPTER 8

Genesis 1:26–27

You and I live on a big planet called the earth. And lots and lots of other people live on it, too. Maybe there are many families on your street and in your town. Well, there are streets and towns just like yours all over the earth. There are so many people we wouldn't be able to count them.

God made this earth and gave us everything we need to live. He provided it for us to enjoy because He loves us. But we must be careful to take care of what He gave us and try to keep it beautiful.

In your town there are probably some people whose skin is a different color from yours, or whose eyes may be a different shape. And maybe you know someone who talks in a language that sounds very funny to you because you don't understand it. They or their families probably come from another country—maybe even the other side of the earth! The earth is a big place.

But with all of those people on the earth, none of them are the same. We are all special in the way we act and the way we look. Do you know what? God made us that way, and He loves us all.

QUESTIONS—CHAPTER 8

1. *What is the name of the planet on which we live?*
2. *Are there lots of people on the earth?*
3. *Who made us?*

Thought Question: What are some things you can do to help keep God's earth beautiful?

Parental Note: In this chapter I wanted to establish an awareness of the need to care for this beautiful world God gave us to enjoy. You may want to further the discussion on practical matters such as not littering, not using extra electricity and consequently using more oil, etc.

This is a photograph of the earth. It looks small because it was taken by an astronaut thousands of miles up in the sky. Can you tell which is the ocean? What do you think the white stuff is?

CHAPTER 9

God made all of the people in the world, and He loves us. He also wants us to love each other and help each other. But because we want to do bad things more than we want to do good things, He gave us a set of rules. These rules are called the Ten Commandments.

1. "You shall have no other gods before me." That means you should love God more than anything or anyone else.
2. "You shall not make for yourself an idol . . . or worship any idol. . . ." That means that you should not make God to look or act like you.
3. "You shall not misuse the name of the Lord." That means that you should always act in such a way that Jesus is glad you are a Christian.
4. "Remember the Sabbath day by keeping it holy." That means that one day of the week should be kept to worship God.
5. "Honor your father and mother. . . ." That means that you must obey your parents and be respectful towards them.
6. "You shall not murder." That means you must respect life.
7. "You shall not commit adultery. . . ." That means when you marry you must love your husband or wife and no one else.
8. "You shall not steal." That means that you must not ever take anything that does not belong to you.
9. "You shall not give false testimony. . . ." That means that you should not lie but always tell the truth.
10. "You shall not covet." That means that you shouldn't want something so badly that you would do anything to get it.

These are very important rules. But no one can keep them perfectly. Only one Person ever kept them and that was Jesus. When we read these rules we see that we need forgiveness for all the times we have done wrong. To ask forgiveness means to say we are sorry and will try not to do the things we have done wrong any more. When we have Jesus in our hearts, God is always ready to forgive us when we ask Him.

QUESTIONS—CHAPTER 9

1. Why did God give us these rules?

2. What are they called?

3. Can you name a few?

4. Who kept all these commandments perfectly?

5. If we know we have done wrong, what can we ask God to do?

6. Will He forgive us?

Thought Question: How can you tell if you love something or someone more than God?

Parental Note: It may seem strange to include a chapter on the Ten Commandments in a book for young children. But in this age in which relativity and situational ethics have been enthroned, it is vital for a child to know that there are some absolutes, some guidelines, and a moral code given by God. My mother uses the illustration of a highway without painted traffic lanes. No one would know where they were supposed to be or go and all would be havoc. So it is morally and spiritually. God has given us a standard of excellence.

CHAPTER 10

God not only made all the different kinds of people in the world to love, but God made wonderful creatures called angels. And do you know what? Everyone who believes in Jesus has an angel all to himself or herself. These angels take care of us; they are called guardian angels.

The angels that are not busy taking care of people live in heaven with God. Angels are very good and always obey God when He tells them to do something.

A very long time ago, there was a little boy named Ishmael. His mother's name was Hagar. They lived in a nice comfortable tent (people lived in tents then), but Ishmael's father sent them away from home. Ishmael and Hagar were sad but they packed their things and left.

They had no place to go, so they wandered out into the wilderness. A wilderness is a place where no one lives, only wild animals and snakes. It isn't a very nice place. It was very hot.

Pretty soon, little Ishmael got thirsty and wanted something to drink. But his mother did not have anything to give him and could not find any water.

Ishmael got very weak and sick. Hagar saw that he was going to die unless he got some water soon. So, she put him under a tree in the shade where it wasn't so hot.

She was very sad and walked out of sight because she didn't want to see him die. She began to cry.

Then God sent an angel to her. The angel asked her, "What is the matter, Hagar? Do not be afraid; God has heard the boy crying as he lies there. Lift the boy up and take him by the hand. . . ." And then do you know what the angel showed her? He showed her where there was some water coming up out of the ground.

So Hagar quickly got Ishmael some water to drink. He got strong and well. He grew up to be a man and lived in the wilderness and learned to shoot with a bow and arrow.

QUESTIONS—CHAPTER 10

1. *What else did God make besides men?*
2. *Where do angels live when they aren't taking care of people?*
3. *What was the name of the little boy in this story?*
4. *Where did Ishmael's mother take him?*
5. *Why did Hagar walk out of sight?*

6. *Why was Ishmael so sick?*
7. *Whom did God send to help Ishmael and Hagar?*
8. *What did the angel show Hagar?*
9. *What happened to Ishmael?*

Thought Question: Why do you think God allowed Ishmael to get so sick?

Parental Note: Until recently the subject of angels was an unfamiliar one. If you would like to find out more about them and what they do, let me refer you to *Angels: God's Secret Agents* by Billy Graham, published 1975 by Doubleday.

Do you see the little boy named Ishmael in this picture? Do you know what Hagar, Ishmael's mother, is doing?

CHAPTER 11

I like stories about angels and how God sends them to help us. Let me tell you a story about angels.

Once there was a very important king. Everyone had to obey him. He had many lions that he kept in a big cage so they couldn't hurt anyone with their sharp teeth and claws.

In the same country there was a very good and wise man named Daniel. But some bad men didn't like Daniel and decided they would try to hurt him.

These bad men talked the king into making a rule that no one could pray to anyone except him. Anyone who did would be put into the lions' cage. But Daniel loved and obeyed God and prayed to Him three times a day openly. Daniel would not pray to the king, so these bad men ran to tell the king that Daniel was praying to someone else.

That made the king sad. The king liked Daniel, but he had made the rule and now Daniel would have to be thrown into the lions' cage. So, the bad men took Daniel and put him in with the lions and shut the door. Daniel could not get out.

This made the king upset and he went home. But he couldn't sleep because he was worried about Daniel. Early in the morning he ran to the lions' cage to see what had happened to Daniel. He called out, "Daniel, servant of the living God, has your God, whom you serve continually, been able to rescue you from the lions?" Daniel answered him, "O king, live forever! My God sent his angel, and he shut the mouths of the lions. They have not hurt me. . . ."

The king was so happy and got Daniel out of the cage. Everyone could see that Daniel was not hurt at all. God had taken care of him.

If we believe in Jesus and try to obey God like Daniel, then God will send angels to take care of us.

QUESTIONS—CHAPTER 11

1. *What animals did the king keep in a cage?*
2. *What was the name of the good man?*
3. *What did the bad men want to do to Daniel?*
4. *What rule did these men talk the king into making?*
5. *Why didn't Daniel obey?*
6. *To whom did Daniel pray?*
7. *What did these men do to Daniel?*

This picture shows Daniel in the cage with the lions.
How many lions do you see? Why didn't the fierce
lions hurt Daniel?

8. *Was the king happy that Daniel was put in the cage with the lions?*
9. *Where did the king go early in the morning?*
10. *What did he see?*
11. *Whom had God sent to help Daniel?*

12. *What did the angels do?*
13. *Will God send an angel to help us if we believe in Jesus?*

Thought Question: Why didn't Daniel pray secretly and try to stay out of trouble?

CHAPTER 12

Remember I told you that angels live in heaven with God? Well, someone else lives there also. The Son of God lives in heaven, too. His name is Jesus. A long time ago, God sent Jesus from heaven to this world where we live. Listen carefully as I tell you about it.

Far away from here, there is a town called Bethlehem. It is a very old town. Many years ago a young woman named Mary came to Bethlehem with her husband, Joseph. They did not live in Bethlehem, so they had to find a place, called an inn, where they could spend the night.

The inn was full of people so that Mary and Joseph could not find a room to spend the night. Joseph was sad and a little worried. He needed to find a place for Mary to be comfortable. She was going to have a baby. A special baby.

They went to the stable where the donkeys and cows stayed. In the stable there is a place for the donkeys and cows to lie down, and there is a place out of which they eat.

When we eat supper, we eat from plates, but donkeys and cows eat out of mangers. There was a manger in the stable where Mary and Joseph had come.

Now it was night and it was not time to feed the animals. But the manger was not empty. There was a brand new baby boy lying in that manger.

When Jesus was born, Mary had no nice cradle to put Him in, so she wrapped Him up in some clothes and put Him into the manger as His cradle.

Do you know what that baby's name was? His name was Jesus. And He was the Son of God.

QUESTIONS—CHAPTER 12

1. *Where does the Son of God live?*
2. *What is His name?*
3. *What is the name of the town where Jesus was born?*
4. *What was Jesus' mother's name?*
5. *What was His father's name?*
6. *Did Mary and Joseph live in Bethlehem?*
7. *Where did Mary and Joseph find a place to sleep?*
8. *Why was Joseph worried?*
9. *What usually sleeps in a stable?*
10. *What was the baby's name?*
11. *Who had sent Jesus to Mary?*
12. *Where did Mary put Jesus?*

Thought Question: Since Jesus was God's own Son, why wasn't He born in a palace or at least a comfortable, clean place?

Parental Note: This chapter begins to establish the deity of Christ which is essential in understanding the Bible.

Children readily accept this and have no problems with it. They may ask why they cannot see Him or what He looks like or how He can live in heaven as well as in their hearts. Keep you answers simple and hontest, such as: we can't see Him because He does not have a body like ours, but one time He did and was seen by people, ate with them, and talked with them. We do not know what He looks like, and we don't know how He can be in two places at one time but He can because the Bible says so.

Do you know what this baby's name was? Why was he born in a stable?

CHAPTER 13

The people who lived in my house before I bought it used to have sheep. They had fenced in the yard and let the sheep eat the grass. That is how they kept the grass mowed!

Well, in the country where Jesus was born, people used to have many sheep. These sheep stayed out in the fields to eat the grass. But since there were wolves and bears in the country that would come into the fields and hurt or kill the sheep, men had to stay in the fields with the sheep to protect and take care of them.

These men were called shepherds. They stayed out in the fields with the sheep all day and especially all night, because when it was dark, the bears and wolves would come to hurt the sheep.

On the night Jesus was born, some shepherds were out in the field taking care of their sheep. And an angel came from heaven and spoke to them. This frightened them, I suppose because they had never seen an angel before.

But the angel told them, "Do not be afraid. I bring you good news of great joy that will be for all people. Today in the town of David a Savior has been born to you." The angel was talking about Jesus and the angel called Jesus the Savior.

QUESTIONS—CHAPTER 13

1. *What kind of animals used to eat the grass in my yard?*
2. *Did the people in the country we have read about have many sheep?*
3. *Where did those sheep go to find grass?*
4. *Why did men have to take care of them?*
5. *What were these men called?*
6. *How long did they stay with the sheep?*
7. *On the night Jesus was born, who came to talk to the shepherds?*
8. *How did the shepherds feel when they saw the angel?*
9. *What did the angel tell them?*
10. *What was the good news?*
11. *What did the angel call Jesus?*

These sheep live in the country where Jesus was born. Do you see the men with the sheep? What do you call men who take care of sheep?

CHAPTER 14

I want to tell you why the angel called Jesus the Savior. Suppose you were playing ball in your yard one afternoon and the ball rolled out into the street. You ran into the street after the ball and did not look to see that a car was coming. The car was coming closer to you at a fast speed and soon would hit you. It would kill you.

But suppose that just then a strong man would run out after you and pick you up and hold you in his arms, and would carry you out of the road to a safe place, so that you would not be hit by the car. That man would save you from the car, wouldn't he?

And Jesus came from heaven to save us, not from a speeding car, but He came to save us from our sins.

Our sins are the bad things we do, like disobeying Mother and Father or lying or being selfish. And Jesus came to save us from doing those bad things, and to save us from being punished for them after we die. That is the reason we call Him our Savior.

Would you like to ask Jesus into your heart?

QUESTIONS—CHAPTER 14

1. *What did the angel call Jesus?*
2. *From what did he come to save us?*
3. *What are our sins? Can you think of some things you have done that have made God unhappy?*
4. *Did Jesus come to save us from doing these bad things?*
5. *If we love Jesus will we be punished for these things after we die?*
6. *What do we call Jesus when He saves us?*

Thought Question: How can Jesus, who died so many years ago, take the punishment for my sins, when I'm alive now?

Parental Note: If your child indicated that he/she understands what sin is, that he/she has sinned and what Jesus has done for and offers in our salvation then you should take advantage of his/her open heart and lead him/her to Jesus through a simple prayer. For a parent, there is no greater joy. Children are the only things we can take to heaven!

A simple prayer that you could use: Dear Jesus, I am sorry for the bad things I have done that make you unhappy. Thank you for dying on the cross and taking my punishment. Please come into my heart to live and help me to be good. Thank you! I love you. In Jesus' Name, Amen.

Imagine what it was like to actually see baby Jesus, the Son of God. This painting from the seventeenth century shows the shepherds kneeling in love at the sight of Jesus.

CHAPTER 15

After the angel had told the shepherds that Jesus was born, he said, "This will be a sign to you: You will find a baby wrapped in strips of cloth and lying in a manger."

Then the shepherds said to one another, "Let's go and see this little child that God has sent His angel to tell us about." So the shepherds left their sheep and quickly went to Bethlehem.

They came into the stable, where they saw Jesus lying in the manger, and they were glad when they saw Him. Afterward they went back to their sheep in the field, and as they went they told all the people what the angel had said to them about Jesus.

QUESTIONS—CHAPTER 15

1. *What did the angel tell the shepherds they could see if they went to Bethlehem?*
2. *What did they do?*
3. *How did the shepherds feel when they saw the baby Jesus?*
4. *What did they do as they went back to their sheep in the field?*

Thought Question: What are some ways you can tell people about Jesus?

Here is another shepherd with his sheep. Doesn't the shepherd's coat look nice and warm?

CHAPTER 16

Some other men came to see Jesus in Bethlehem. They were called "wise men." These wise men knew a great deal about the stars. They used to stay up all night sometimes, looking at the stars, trying to learn all about them.

One night when they were looking up at the sky, they saw a new star that was different from all the stars they had ever seen before. God had sent that star for the wise men to see, so they might know His Son was born.

As soon as they knew that Jesus was born they wanted to see Him. So they thought they would go and find Him, but they lived a great way from Bethlehem. They did not know where Bethlehem was, and how would they find the way? I will tell you. God made the star that they had seen up in the sky go before them and show them the way to Bethlehem.

They followed the star and came to Bethlehem and there they saw Jesus. They knelt down on the ground in front of Him and worshiped Him. Then they took out some presents they had brought and gave them to Him. Afterward they went back to their own homes.

QUESTIONS—CHAPTER 16

1. *Who else came to see Jesus in Bethlehem?*
2. *What did they know a great deal about?*
3. *One night when they were looking up at the sky, what did they see?*
4. *Who had sent that star?*
5. *Why did God send the star for the wise men to see?*
6. *After they had seen the star what did they want to do?*
7. *How did they find their way to Bethlehem?*
8. *What did they do when they saw Jesus?*
9. *Where did they go afterwards?*

Thought Question: How does God lead us to Jesus today?

Who are these men? Where are they going? How will they find the way? Do you know what animals they are riding?

CHAPTER 17

There was a king in that country. Remember, I told you that the king was the man that everybody had to obey? But this king that I am telling you about now was very wicked. When he heard about Jesus, he was very jealous and wanted to kill Him. So he sent some men to Bethlehem to kill all the baby boys who were there. And the men did go to Bethlehem and kill all the baby boys, but they did not kill Jesus.

They did not kill Jesus, because God sent an angel down from heaven to tell Joseph that the men were coming. The angel came to Joseph while he was asleep, and said, "Get up, take the Child and His mother and escape to Egypt. Stay there until I tell you, for Herod is going to search for the Child to kill Him."

So Joseph got up in the night while it was dark so no one would see him, and he took the Child Jesus and Mary, His mother, and went away to another country called Egypt, where the king's men could not find Him.

After a while the wicked king died, and then Joseph brought Jesus and Mary back to their own country. They came to a city called Nazareth. Jesus lived in Nazareth for many years, until He grew up to be a man. But the people did not know He was God's Son, for no one had told them this yet.

QUESTIONS—CHAPTER 17

1. *What did the king send some men to Bethlehem to do?*
2. *Why did he send men to kill all the little children in Bethlehem?*
3. *What did the men do?*
4. *Did they kill Jesus?*
5. *Who had told Joseph to take Jesus away?*
6. *Where did he take Jesus and Mary, His mother?*
7. *What happened to the wicked king after a while?*
8. *What did Joseph do then?*
9. *Where did they go to live?*
10. *How long did Jesus live in Nazareth?*

Thought Question: Do you sometimes get jealous? What do you do about it?

This is what Mary and Joseph might have looked like. There were no cars when Jesus lived. People had to walk or ride on donkeys.

CHAPTER 18

There was a young man in that same country who was just a little older than Jesus. His name was John the Baptist. He was Jesus' cousin and was a very good man. He didn't live in a town, but instead he lived in the wilderness. Remember I told you that a wilderness is a place where no one lives but the wild animals and snakes? John the Baptist lived there all by himself.

John wore a very strange coat. It was made of camel's hair. Camels live in countries that are very hot, and often you find them near desert places where there is little or no water. God made camels so that they can go a long time, four or five days, without water, even when they are carrying heavy loads on their backs.

Have you ever seen a camel? They are very strange looking animals. They have long necks and funny-looking faces and big humps on their backs. Their bodies are covered with hair and people would cut the hair off to make clothes out of it. The coat of John the Baptist was made of camels' hair.

John not only wore a very strange coat, but he ate unusual food. He did not eat meat and potatoes or bread as you and I do. Instead, he ate locusts and wild honey. Locusts are insects that look very much like grasshoppers. There are lots of them in the part of the world where John lived, and the people eat them for food. They roast the locusts over the fire, put salt on them, and they are ready to eat.

John also ate honey. Remember I told you that bees make honey? They go from flower to flower collecting nectar to take back to their hives.

There were bees out in the wilderness with John the Baptist. But they didn't have hives. Instead, they would make their honey in holes in the trees or rocks. John used to find the honey and eat it.

John was a very good man; he loved God and obeyed God. God told John to leave the wilderness to tell the people about Jesus. He was to teach them that Jesus was God's Son. Now the time had come for people to be told about this.

John went to a place near a river— the river Jordan. It was a big river. Many people came to hear what John had to say. John told them that very soon they would see Jesus and that they must get ready.

How were they to get ready? Were they to put on their best clothes? No, that is not what John meant. The way to get ready for Jesus was to stop doing everything that was wrong and not to do it any more and ask God to take away their sins.

QUESTIONS—CHAPTER 18

1. *What was the name of the good man?*
2. *Where did he live?*
3. *What was his coat made of?*
4. *Where do camels live?*
5. *What do people make out of camels' hair?*
6. *What did John the Baptist eat?*
7. *What did God tell him to do?*
8. *What was the name of the big river John came to?*

9. *Did many people come to hear what he said?*
10. *What did John tell them?*
11. *How were they to get ready?*

Thought Question: Why do you think John lived in the wilderness?

Parental Note: I introduce in this chapter a bit of Biblical cultural background. This helps establish the Bible as a historical book with real people and real events.

John the Baptist wore a coat made of camel's hair. Which is the camel in this picture?

CHAPTER 19

Some of the people who listened to John obeyed him and stopped doing wrong things. But others didn't pay any attention to him. John took the people who obeyed him down to the river Jordan to baptize them.

Do you know what it means to be baptized? It means that we are sorry for all the wrong things we have done and have asked Jesus to forgive us. It is a way of saying to everyone that Jesus has washed away our sins and we have asked Him to live in our hearts.

While John was baptizing all the people at the river, Jesus came and asked John to baptize Him. And John did baptize Jesus.

Jesus' baptism was very special, because Jesus never did anything wrong so there was really no need to "wash away" any sins. He asked to be baptized to say that the preaching of John was right and that soon Jesus was going to truly wash away our sins by His blood.

When Jesus came up out of the water after being baptized, a wonderful thing happened. He heard a voice from heaven speaking. It was God's voice, and God was saying, "This is My Son, Whom I love; with Him I am well pleased."

Just then a beautiful bird flew down and rested on Jesus. It looked like a dove, but it wasn't. It was the Holy Spirit.

QUESTIONS—CHAPTER 19

1. *Where did John take the people who obeyed him?*
2. *What did he do at the river?*
3. *What is baptism?*
4. *Who came to John to be baptized?*
5. *When Jesus came out of the water, whose voice did He hear?*
6. *What did God say?*
7. *What flew down and rested on Jesus?*
8. *Who was it?*

Thought Question: How and when does the Holy Spirit come to us today?

Parental Note: Here is introduced the person of the Holy Spirit. If your child shows interest, a discussion as to who the Holy Spirit is and what He does (we cannot see Him but He helps us obey God) will help your child in an important but often neglected subject. If you are unclear in your own mind about the Holy Spirit, I suggest you refer to *The Holy Spirit* by Billy Graham published 1978 by Word Books, Publisher, Waco, Texas.

Do you know what it means to be baptized? What are
these men doing in the water with their clothes on?
Would you like Jesus to wash away all your sins, and
forgive you for the wrong things you've done?

The Holy Spirit then led Jesus out in the wilderness. But the wild animals and snakes who lived there would not hurt Jesus because He was the Son of God.

He stayed out in the wilderness a long time—forty days and nights. He didn't have anything to eat or drink the whole time. Afterward, He was very hungry.

While Jesus was out in the wilderness, Satan came to Him; he came to try to get Jesus to do wrong. Remember, Satan was the one who made Eve disobey God. He tries very hard to make us do wrong. He is very bad.

Satan knew that Jesus was hungry and that He wanted bread to eat; so Satan told Jesus to change the stones that were lying on the ground into bread. Jesus could easily have changed the stones into bread, but He would not do it, because that would be obeying Satan.

Then Satan took Jesus away from the wilderness to a very high place on the top of a beautiful church called the temple. And Satan told Jesus to throw Himself down from that high place, for Satan said that God would send some angels to catch Him while He was falling, so that He would not be hurt when He fell.

But Jesus would not do this, either, because to obey Satan would be wrong.

Then Satan took Jesus on to a very high hill or mountain, and he showed Jesus a great many beautiful countries and cities from that high mountain. Jesus could see them all at the same time.

Satan told Jesus that if He would only obey him He would have all those beautiful countries and cities for His own. But Jesus said that He would obey God, and He would not mind Satan, for God says in the Bible that He is the One we must obey.

When Satan found that Jesus would not obey him, Satan went away and left Jesus. Then some good angels came and took care of Jesus.

Sometimes Satan comes to us and tries to make us do bad things. We cannot see him when he comes, but we can tell he is near, for he makes us feel as if we want to do wrong.

But when we feel like doing wrong things, let us tell Satan that we will not do wrong. Then he will go away from us, as he went away from Jesus.

Why did Jesus refuse to turn the stones into bread? If you hadn't eaten for forty days and nights, wouldn't this bread be tempting?

QUESTIONS—CHAPTER 20

1. *Where did Jesus go after His baptism?*
2. *How long did He stay in the wilderness?*
3. *Did He eat or drink anything?*

4. *Who came into the wilderness to try and make Jesus do wrong?*
5. *Into what did Satan tell Jesus to change the stones?*
6. *Could Jesus have changed the stones into bread?*
7. *But would He obey Satan?*
8. *When Satan took Jesus up to a high place on the temple, what did he want Jesus to do?*
9. *Who did Satan say would come and catch Jesus to keep Him from being hurt when He fell?*
10. *Would Jesus throw Himself down from the top of the temple to obey Satan?*
11. *What did Satan show Jesus from the top of the mountain?*
12. *What did Satan promise Jesus?*
13. *But who did Jesus say He would obey?*
14. *What book tells us we must obey God?*
15. *When Satan found that Jesus wouldn't obey him, what did he do?*
16. *Who came then and took care of Jesus?*
17. *Does Satan ever come to us and try to make us do wrong?*
18. *Can we see him when he comes?*
19. *How can we tell he is near us?*
20. *What should we say to him when he tries to make us do wrong?*

Thought Question: Is temptation a sin?

CHAPTER 21

When Jesus left the wilderness, He went to a town called Cana. In this town there was a man who had just gotten married. This man was giving a big dinner for his friends to celebrate his wedding. All kinds of fine foods were made for the dinner for them to eat, and there were good wines for them to drink.

Wine is made from grapes. In that country, people used to grow lots of grapes. People used to make wine from those grapes. So, this man served wine to his friends at dinner.

But so many people came to his dinner that soon all the wine was gone. They asked for more, but there wasn't any more.

Jesus was at the dinner and so was His mother, Mary. Mary noticed that all the man's wine was gone, so she took the man's servants to Jesus and told them, "Do whatever He tells you."

Jesus told the servants to bring in some water and to pour it into some great tall jars. There were six tall jars standing on the floor of the dining room. The servants obeyed Jesus and filled the jars up to the top with water.

Then Jesus told them, "Now draw some out and take it to the master of the banquet." The man tasted it and found out that it wasn't water now. It was wine. Jesus had changed the water into wine.

Jesus hadn't touched the wine or put anything into it. He had only told them to "draw some out and take it to the master of the banquet." The man tasted it and found out that it wasn't water now. It was wine. Jesus had changed the water into wine. That was a miracle.

The water obeyed Jesus because He is the Son of God, and He can do the same things God can do.

QUESTIONS—CHAPTER 21

1. *What was the name of the town Jesus went to?*
2. *What had just happened?*
3. *Who was giving the party?*
4. *What was he serving to drink?*
5. *What happened?*
6. *Who was at the party?*
7. *What did Mary tell the servants to do?*
8. *What did Jesus tell them to do?*
9. *What did they do?*
10. *When the man tasted the water, what had happened?*
11. *Who had changed the water into wine?*
12. *What was that called?*

13. Why could Jesus do miracles?

Thought Question: Do you think that while Jesus was here on earth, He laughed and had fun?

Parental Note: Here is some more Biblical cultural background. Also, this Scripture helps us see whether Jesus had a sense of humor or was always encumbered by His ministry. Here He was at a wedding party. He enjoyed people and laughed. He is not stern, always demanding of us. He accepts us just the way we are. He does not hand us a list of don'ts—He gave us all things to enjoy, under authority of Scripture.

Which man do you think is Jesus? How many water jars can you see? What did Jesus turn the water into?

CHAPTER 22

John the Baptist was a great preacher. He would tell the people to stop doing wrong and to ask God to forgive them. In that same country, there was a very bad king, named Herod, who was doing something very bad. He was living with a woman who was not his wife. John told him to quit and that made the woman very mad so she had John thrown into prison.

While John was in prison, Herod had a birthday. He gave a big birthday party for himself and invited many friends who came to eat and drink. While they were eating and drinking, a young woman came into the room. Her name was Salome. She could dance very well, so she danced for King Herod and his friends. This made the king very happy. It made him so happy that he promised to give her anything she wanted.

Salome went to her mother and asked what she should tell the king she wanted. Her wicked mother told her to ask the king to kill John the Baptist.

So Salome went back to the party, which was still going on, and told the king that she wanted him to have John the Baptist killed.

The king knew that this was wrong. He knew that John was a good man and did not deserve to be killed; yet to make Salome and her wicked mother happy, he sent a man into the prison to kill John.

After John was killed, some good men who loved John went to the prison and got John's body. They took it to a grave and buried it.

QUESTIONS—CHAPTER 22

1. *What was the name of the king in the story?*
2. *What did John tell the king to quit doing?*
3. *What did Herod do to John?*
4. *Whose birthday was it?*
5. *Who came to dance at the party?*
6. *What did Herod say to her?*
7. *What did her mother tell Salome to ask for?*
8. *Did Herod know it would be wrong to kill John?*
9. *What happened?*
10. *Why did he do it?*

Thought Question: Do you sometimes do something wrong because you want to be accepted by your friends?

Parental Note: The Bible teaches that it is wrong to live with one of the opposite sex without marriage. It is good to start now to gently begin to teach God's plan for marriage as opposed to the current lifestyles open to our children which God condemns. Don't be heavy-handed; simply make marriage attractive. Emphasize the positive side. The world is very subtle in undermining marriage; we can be just as subtle in building it up.

Why did Herod have John thrown into prison? When you ask Jesus to come into your heart, His love can reach you anywhere—even through prison bars.

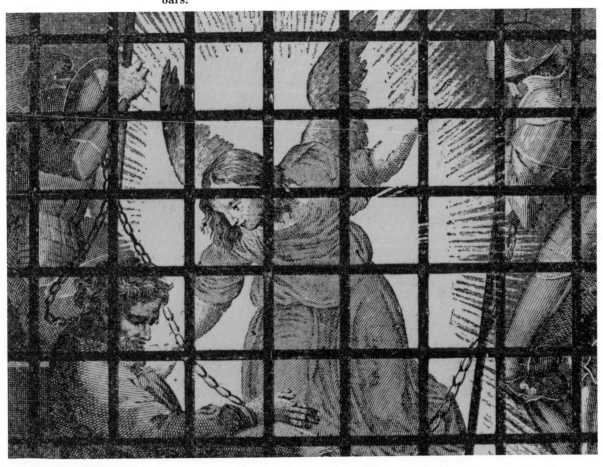

CHAPTER 23

Jesus went back to the town named Cana where He had changed the water into wine. There was a very rich man who lived in Cana. His son was very sick. The doctors could not make him well, even though they had tried many medicines. His father was afraid the little boy would die.

When he heard that Jesus was in Cana he hurried to see Him. He begged Jesus to make his son well. He told Jesus, "Sir, come down before my child dies." The man thought that Jesus would have to come home with him to see his son before Jesus could make his son well.

But Jesus told the man, "You may go. Your son will live." The man believed what Jesus said and went back home. On his way home, his servants came out to meet the man to tell him that his son was already well.

Jesus had made him well by just saying so, for as soon as Jesus said that, the sickness left the little boy and he was well. This was a miracle.

QUESTIONS—CHAPTER 23

1. *What town had Jesus gone back to?*
2. *What did the rich man ask Jesus to do?*
3. *Could the doctors make his son well?*
4. *What did the rich man think Jesus had to do to make his son well?*
5. *What did Jesus say to him?*
6. *On his way home, what did the man's servants come out to tell him?*
7. *Who made his son well?*
8. *How had Jesus made the little boy well?*
9. *What was this?*

Thought Question: Why didn't Jesus go to the man's house and heal the young boy there?

This picture is of Bethlehem, a town very like the town of Cana in the story. Try to imagine what it was like to live in a house like these.

CHAPTER 24

Then Jesus came to another town named Capernaum. It was very near the Sea of Galilee. Jesus liked to walk on the beach and many people followed Him and crowded around Him.

Jesus saw two boats on the beach; they belonged to men who used them to sail out onto the sea and catch fish. But these men were not out catching fish. Instead, they were mending their nets. Nets are like big open-weave blankets made of string and rope. They are used for catching fish.

If you have ever gone fishing, you probably took a long pole with a line and hook and a few worms. But you only caught one fish at a time. If you used a net like these men you would catch a lot of fish at a time. That's why they used the nets instead of poles.

When the people crowded around Jesus on the beach, He got into one of the boats and asked the man who owned it to go out on the water just a little way. The man did what Jesus asked. So, Jesus sat down and talked to the people as they stood on the beach.

When Jesus finished talking to the people, He told the man, "Put out into deep water, and let down the nets for a catch." But the man said, "Master, we've worked hard all night and haven't caught anything. But because you say so, I will let down the nets." This man's name was Peter.

So Peter and his brother took their oars and rowed out on the sea. They let down their mended net, but when they tried to pull it back up into the boat, it was so full of fish they couldn't lift it.

Peter called out to some men on the beach to come help them. These men also had a boat, so they came and helped Peter and his brother pull up the net. When they had pulled it up and put the fish into the boats, the boats were so full of fish that they were close to sinking.

It was Jesus who made the fish come to the spot where the men could catch them. The men had tried to catch them before, but the fish were not there. But when Jesus told them to try, so many fish came that the boats were full.

This was a miracle. Jesus did this on purpose to show these men that He was God's Son.

Then Jesus told these men to follow Him. They immediately left their boats and nets and all that they had to follow Jesus. From then on they stayed with Jesus all the time.

QUESTIONS—CHAPTER 24

1. *What was the town of Capernaum close to?*
2. *Who liked to walk on the beach?*
3. *What happened when Jesus walked on the beach?*
4. *Who did Jesus see on the beach?*
5. *What were the men doing?*
6. *Why weren't they fishing?*
7. *What was the name of the man who owned the boat?*
8. *What had he and his brother done all night?*
9. *When Jesus told them to fish, what happened?*
10. *What do we call this?*
11. *Why did Jesus do this?*
12. *Did these men follow Jesus?*

Thought Question: Pretend you were in Peter's boat that day. How would you have felt and acted?

When you go fishing you probably use a long pole with a line and hook and a few worms. In the story, the men used big fishing nets like the one in the picture.

CHAPTER 25

Then Jesus went to the house where Peter lived. Remember Peter was the fisherman who followed Jesus? There was a woman in the house who was very sick. She had a high fever and was lying in bed. The other people in the house asked Jesus to make her well.

So, Jesus went to the side of her bed and told the fever to go away. And do you know what? It did! The fever went away and she was well. Jesus took her hand and told her to get up. She got up and began serving the people who were in the house.

Around town, the news of what Jesus had done spread, so that evening when it began to get dark, many people brought their sick friends to Jesus so He could make them well. And He tenderly made them all well.

Jesus stayed at Peter's house all night.

QUESTIONS—CHAPTER 25

1. *Whose house did Jesus go to?*
2. *What was wrong with the woman in the house?*
3. *What did Jesus do for her?*
4. *When Jesus told the fever to go away, what happened?*
5. *When people heard about it, what did they do?*
6. *What did Jesus do?*

Parental Note: For a deeper understanding of healing today refer to *The Holy Spirit* by Billy Graham, published 1978 by Word Books, Publisher, Waco, Texas.

Peter's house was in a town just like this one.

CHAPTER 26

Early the next morning before the sun was up, Jesus woke up and went out of Peter's house to the wilderness. He wanted to be alone so that He could pray to God, His Father.

After Jesus had left Peter's house, the people from the town came to look for Him. When they heard that He had gone into the wilderness they went out to find Him. When they found Him, they begged Him to stay in their town and not to leave.

But Jesus said, "I must preach the good news of the Kingdom of God to the other towns also, because that is why I was sent." God had sent Jesus to our world to show us that God loves us. But because we have done many bad things, called sins, we have to repent and ask God to forgive us. To repent is to be sorry for something you have done—so sorry that you want never to do it again. So Jesus went to many towns to tell the people these things.

QUESTIONS—CHAPTER 26

1. *Where did Jesus go very early in the morning?*
2. *Why did He go into the wilderness?*
3. *Who went out to find Jesus?*
4. *When they found Him, what did they want Him to do?*
5. *What did Jesus say to them?*
6. *What does repent mean?*
7. *What are sins?*

Thought Question: Do you follow Jesus' example of getting alone to pray?

Parental Note: This chapter introduces the doctrines of repentance and forgiveness. At this point you might want to ask your child if he/she wants to ask Jesus to forgive him/her for his/her sins and come into his/her heart.

Do you sometimes get up very early in the morning? Doesn't the sun look beautiful?

CHAPTER 27

Luke 5:12–15

A long time ago, my grandfather took me to visit a hospital where people were very, very sick. It was a certain sickness that made sores come on a person's skin and turn it as white as snow. Sometimes the sickness was so bad that the person would lose his or her fingers or hands or feet or nose or ears. It wasn't a very nice thing to see.

This same sickness, called leprosy, made people sick in the country where Jesus lived. When a person got leprosy he would have to leave his home and go to a place by himself so that his family would not get sick with leprosy. They didn't have nice hospitals then for those people to go to. They would go away from their homes and could not come back until they were well. But no one could make them well except God.

When Jesus was walking in a town one day, a poor man who had leprosy came to Jesus. He knelt down on the ground in front of Jesus and said, "Lord, if you are willing, you can make me clean." Jesus felt sad. He didn't like to see such a sick man suffering. Jesus said, "I am willing." He then told the man, "Be clean." As soon as Jesus said that, the leprosy went away and the man was well.

The man was so happy and excited that he went out and told everyone he saw how Jesus had made him well. After that, so many people came to Jesus and crowded around Him that He could not stay there any more.

QUESTIONS—CHAPTER 27

1. *What bad sickness did I tell you about in this story?*
2. *When a person got leprosy, could he stay with his family?*
3. *Who can make a person well?*
4. *What did the man with the leprosy ask Jesus to do for him?*
5. *Did Jesus do it?*
6. *What did the man do?*
7. *What did the people do?*

Thought Question: Why was Jesus willing to heal the man with leprosy?

Parental Note: Again there is some cultural background. Leprosy shouldn't upset a child. Explain that it is not common today and medicines are available to help cure it. Emphasize the love and power of Jesus.

When Jesus healed the sick man, crowds of people
began to follow Jesus wherever He went. Why do
you think they all wanted to come close to Jesus?

CHAPTER 28

After this, Jesus went back to the town called Capernaum. There were many houses in that town but they did not look like the houses you and I live in. They were small, square houses that were only one story high. The roofs on these houses were flat so that a person could go up and walk around on them.

Jesus was in one of these houses teaching the people who had come to see Him. In the same town, there was a man who was very sick with a disease called palsy. Some of his friends wanted to take this man to Jesus, but the man was so sick and weak he could not walk.

So they decided that they would pick up the bed he was lying on and carry him to Jesus. But when they got to the house where Jesus was, there were so many people crowded around the door to listen to Jesus, that they could not get through.

This man's friends carried him up onto the flat roof of the house and opened up a hole in the roof. Then they lowered the sick man on his bed very carefully into the room where Jesus was.

When Jesus saw how much trouble these men had gone to to bring their sick friend to Him, He was happy. He said to the sick man, "I tell you, get up, take your mat and go home." Just by saying that Jesus had made the man well.

The man had been so sick that he couldn't even stand up, much less carry his own bed. But now Jesus had made him well and he could walk, run, and carry his bed all the way home.

When the people who had crowded the house and doorway saw this, they were surprised and said to each other, "We have seen a wonderful thing today."

QUESTIONS—CHAPTER 28

1. *What were the houses like in Capernaum?*
2. *When Jesus was teaching in one of these houses, who was brought to Him?*
3. *Why couldn't the man's friends get him through the door?*
4. *Where did they carry him?*
5. *When the men made a hole in the roof, what did they do with the sick man?*
6. *Why was Jesus happy?*
7. *What did Jesus tell the man to do?*
8. *How did Jesus make him well?*

Thought Question: Would you go to a lot of trouble to bring a friend to Him?

In Capernaum the houses did not look like the
houses you and I live in. They looked like the houses
in this picture. Pretend that you live in one of them.
What would it be like?

Parental Note: Again some cultural background. Point
out the houses in the photograph that have flat roofs. Point
out to the child that people in another part of the world
still live in houses like that.

CHAPTER 29

John 5:2–15

MEMORY VERSE—John 14:1 **"Do not let your hearts be troubled. Trust in God; trust also in me."**

The cities in Jesus' country had very high, thick walls all around them. These walls were there to protect the city from robbers or enemies or anyone else that would come to hurt the people in the city.

There was a very important big city named Jerusalem. It had a high, thick wall all the way around it, and the only way you could get inside Jerusalem was to walk through one of the seven gates that went through the wall. If you visit Jerusalem today, you can see that wall and the gates that go through it.

One of these gates was called the sheep gate. It was called the sheep gate because the people would take sheep into the city through this particular gate. Near the sheep gate was a pool of water called the Pool of Bethesda.

Sometimes the water in the pool would begin to move and have ripples on it as if someone were swimming in it. But the people could not see anyone going into it. They thought it was probably an angel who went into the pool and made the water move and ripple. When this happened, if a sick person got into the water, they thought he would get well.

Many people used to sit by the pool. Some were blind and could not see; some were lame and could not walk; some were weak and sick, lying on their beds. They were all waiting for the water to move so that they could try to get into the water quickly and be made well.

On Sunday Jesus came to the pool and saw all the sick people who were waiting there. One of these people was a man who had been sick a long time. Jesus knew how long without even asking, because He knows all about us.

The man was lying on his bed and could not get up. Jesus went over to him and asked, "Do you want to get well?" The man said, "Sir, I have no one to help me into the pool when the water is stirred. While I am trying to get in, someone else goes down ahead of me."

Jesus told the man, "Get up! Pick up your mat and walk." Immediately the man did what Jesus told him to do and was well.

Some people nearby criticized Jesus for making this man well on Sunday. But Jesus told them that God had sent Him to do these things.

Do you know what this gateway into Jerusalem is called? Why are the walls to the city so high and thick?

QUESTIONS—CHAPTER 29

1. *What was built around cities in that country?*

2. *How could you get through the wall into the city?*
3. *What was one of the gates of Jerusalem called?*
4. *What was nearby the sheep gate?*
5. *Who did the people think made the water move?*
6. *If a sick person went into the pool when the water moved, what did they think would happen to that person?*
7. *Were many people waiting by the pool for the water to move?*
8. *What did the man tell Jesus?*
9. *What did Jesus tell him to do?*
10. *Was the man able to stand up and carry his bed when Jesus told him to?*
11. *Why did some people criticize Jesus for making him well?*
12. *Who sent Jesus to do these things?*

Thought Question: When there were probably so many people at the Pool of Bethesda, why do you think Jesus picked this man out?

Parental Note: The cultural background in this chapter is to underline the historicity of the people, places, and events of the Bible. You might want to get out a map and point out where Jerusalem is—a lesson in geography as well!

CHAPTER 30

Jesus told the people who were listening to Him that they should read the Bible, because the Bible is the book that tells about Him.

Suppose you had done wrong, and your father was angry with you and was going to punish you, but your brother was sorry for you, and he came and asked to be punished in your place. Wouldn't that show how much your brother loved you?

This is what Jesus did for us. We have done wrong, and God was going to punish us; but Jesus loved us so much that He came down from heaven to be punished in our place. The Bible is the book that tells us about this.

QUESTIONS—CHAPTER 30

1. *What book did Jesus tell the people to read?*
2. *If you were going to be punished for doing wrong, and your brother would come and ask to be punished in your place, what would that show?*
3. *When God was going to punish us, what did Jesus do?*
4. *Why did He do this?*
5. *What is the book that tells us about this?*

Thought Question: Do you have a time each day when you read the Bible?

Parental Note: This chapter underlines the substitutionary atonement of Jesus. This is a key ingredient to our faith.

The Bible is the most famous book ever written. Bibles come in all shapes, sizes and colors. Have you read about Jesus in your Bible?

Jesus went into a church on Sunday, and many people were there. In that day Sunday was called the Sabbath and a church was called a temple or a synagogue. One of the men in the temple had something wrong with his hand. He could not shut or open his hand as you can, because it was stiff and withered up as if it were dead.

This poor man was not able to work with his hand and earn money to buy bread for his little children. When Jesus saw him, He was sad.

But some men in the temple said that Jesus ought not to make the man well then, because that day was the Sabbath. They said that God had told them not to work on the Sabbath.

Then Jesus spoke to these men and said, "If any of you has a sheep and it falls into a pit on the Sabbath, will you not take hold of it and lift it out? How much more valuable is a man than a sheep! Therefore, it is lawful to do good on the Sabbath."

So Jesus taught the men who found fault with Him that it is right to be kind to persons who are poor and sick on the Sabbath. Then Jesus said to the man, "Stretch out your hand." At once the man's hand was made well, and he could stretch it out like the other.

Before that time he could not move it at all, but Jesus had made it strong and well by speaking those few words. Now the man could go and work and earn bread for his little children to eat.

QUESTIONS—CHAPTER 31

1. *What place did Jesus go into on Sunday?*
2. *What was wrong with the man there?*
3. *Was this poor man able to work and earn bread for his little children?*
4. *Why did some persons say that Jesus shouldn't cure the man then?*
5. *What did Jesus ask them?*
6. *What should we do for the poor and sick?*
7. *What did Jesus say to the man with the withered hand?*
8. *What happened?*

This picture shows a model of a beautiful church. What do you call this kind of church?

CHAPTER 32

After this Jesus went back into the wilderness to pray to God, His Father. Jesus prayed all night long. In the morning, He called twelve of the disciples who had come to hear Him; He chose these men to stay with Him all the time. They were to listen to Him and learn from Him. They were to go wherever He sent them and do whatever He said.

These twelve men Jesus called "apostles." I want you to remember this: the twelve men who stayed with Jesus all the time were called "apostles."

Then Jesus went up on a hillside and many people followed Him there to learn what He had to teach them. Jesus taught them what they should do to please God. He told them that they should not be proud and think that they are better than other people. Instead, they must think of things to help other people and remember how often they had done something wrong and they must be sorry for doing it.

He told the people that they must be kind to each other and to helpless animals. Sometimes little children are cruel and hurt helpless animals, but God is not happy with them when they do that.

Jesus said that the people must not argue and fight with each other or be angry at each other. And when someone is unkind to them, they must not be unkind back but must be kind to them and pray for them.

And Jesus told the people that they must always try to obey God.

QUESTIONS—CHAPTER 32

1. *How long did Jesus stay out in the wilderness praying?*
2. *In the morning, how many men did He call to stay with Him all the time and learn from Him?*
3. *What were these men called?*
4. *What did Jesus tell the people on the hillside?*
5. *Should people be proud and think they are better than other people?*
6. *How should people act toward each other?*
7. *How were they to treat helpless animals?*
8. *If someone is unkind to us, what should we do?*
9. *Who did Jesus say we must try to obey all the time?*

Thought Question: What are some things you can do this week to help your family or friends?

Parental Note: Children have very tender hearts but can be very unkind to each other. You might point out a practical application of this chapter by saying, "Remember when Susie took your ball, and you hit her? What do you think Jesus would have had you do?"

Jesus tells us to be kind to other people and to helpless animals. When people love each other and are
kind to each other, God is happy.

CHAPTER 33

Again, Jesus came to the town of Capernaum. A man lived there who was a soldier. This soldier had a man who worked for him and the soldier loved him very much. But this man was very sick. The soldier was afraid that this man would die.

So the soldier came to Jesus and said, "Lord, my servant lies at home paralyzed and in terrible suffering." Jesus told the soldier, "I will go and heal him." But the soldier replied, "Lord, I do not deserve to have You come under my roof. But just say the word, and my servant will be healed. For I myself am a man under authority, with soldiers under me. I tell this one 'go' and he goes; and that one 'come' and he comes. I say to my servant, 'do this' and he does it."

Jesus was happy that the soldier believed that Jesus could make the man well by just saying so. Jesus told the soldier, "Go, it will be done just as you believed it would."

So the soldier went back home and found that the sickness had left the man. He was already well, just as Jesus had said.

QUESTIONS—CHAPTER 33

1. *Who came to Jesus when He was in Capernaum?*
2. *Did the soldier love the man who worked for him?*
3. *What was wrong with this man?*
4. *What did the soldier want Jesus to do?*
5. *Why was Jesus happy?*
6. *When the soldier got home, what did he find?*

Thought Question: How do you think the soldier knew that Jesus could heal his servant?

Do you think this servant and his master love each other as much as the soldier and servant in the story?

CHAPTER 34

Remember I told you that the towns had a high wall around them for protection? Jesus went to another town that had a wall around it. This town was called Nain. The wall around Nain also had gates so that people could go in and out.

As Jesus came near to the town He met some men coming out of the gate. They were carrying a dead man on a stretcher. They were carrying him out of the town to bury him in a grave.

This dead man was the only son that his mother had ever had and she was a widow; her husband had already died, so she was alone. She was walking beside the stretcher to her son's grave. She was very sad and was crying. She did not think she would ever see her son again.

When Jesus saw this woman crying, He was sorry for her and said to her, "Don't cry." Then He went over beside the stretcher where her son lay and He touched it. The men carrying the stretcher stopped.

Jesus spoke to the dead man. He said, "Young man, I say to you, get up!" As soon as Jesus said that the dead man came to life again. He opened his eyes, sat up, and began to talk. The man and his mother were together again and so happy.

When the people saw the dead man come to life, they were filled with wonder and praised God. They said that surely Jesus had been sent from God because no one but God's Son could bring a man back to life.

QUESTIONS—CHAPTER 34

1. *When Jesus got close to the town of Nain, who was being carried out of the gate?*
2. *Why was his mother crying?*
3. *When Jesus saw her crying, what did He tell her?*
4. *When Jesus went beside the stretcher, what did He say to the dead man?*
5. *What happened then?*
6. *How did the people feel when they saw the dead man come to life?*
7. *Who did they say had sent Jesus to them?*

Thought Question: As far as we know, God doesn't raise people from the dead in these days, but can you think of any miracles He does perform?

These men are carrying a man on a stretcher. Probably they look a lot like the men Jesus met as He came near the town of Nain.

CHAPTER 35

In the country where Jesus lived the people used to buy a very nice lotion, called ointment. They would use the ointment to rub on their hair and skin to make it soft and smooth. It smelled very sweet, like pretty flowers.

One day a man asked Jesus to come to his house for dinner. So Jesus went there and sat down to dinner. In that country, instead of having tables and chairs in the dining room, they had a very low table and sat or reclined on big pillows. Also, instead of shoes, the people usually wore sandals because it was very hot and the roads were dusty.

While Jesus was eating dinner at this man's house, a woman came into the dining room. In her hand she had a little box of ointment. It had cost her a lot of money.

She went over to Jesus and broke the box and poured all of the ointment on Jesus' feet. Then she knelt down and kissed His feet and began to wipe His feet with her hair. She did this to show how very much she loved Jesus. She loved Him because He had come from heaven to be her Savior.

Remember I told you what a Savior was. I told you a story to help you understand it. I said, Suppose you were running after a ball and ran into the street. You didn't see a car coming but a man nearby did, and he ran out and pulled you out of the street just in time. That man would have saved you from being killed by the car.

In the same way, Jesus came from heaven to save this woman from her sins.

She had made God unhappy by doing many bad things, but now she was truly sorry for her sins and didn't want to do them any more. Jesus told her that this made God happy and He would not punish her. When Jesus did this, He was her Savior, and she loved Him for coming from heaven to save her from her sins.

The story tells how a woman washed Jesus' feet with expensive lotion, called ointment. Do you know why she did that?

QUESTIONS—CHAPTER 35

1. *What did the people use to buy to put on their hair and skin?*
2. *While Jesus was eating dinner, who came into the room?*
3. *What did this woman have in her hand?*
4. *Where did she pour the ointment from the box?*
5. *What did she do to His feet?*
6. *Had she done many wrong things and made God unhappy with her?*
7. *Was she sorry for them now?*
8. *When Jesus forgave her what was He to her?*
9. *Did she love Him because He forgave her?*

Thought Question: Would you give something to Jesus that cost you a lot of money?

CHAPTER 36

MEMORY VERSE—Matthew 5:16 "In the same way, let your light shine before men, that they may see your good deeds and praise your Father in heaven."

One day some people brought to Jesus a man who was blind and could not speak. To be blind means a person cannot see anything, but everything is always dark. You can see your friends' faces and the sun shining, but this man couldn't see anything. You can laugh and talk to your friends, but this man couldn't.

When Jesus saw this man, He was sorry for him and made him well. How happy this must have made the man when he opened his eyes and found that he could see—and when he opened his mouth and found that he could talk to his friends whom he loved.

QUESTIONS—CHAPTER 36

1. *What was wrong with the man in this story?*
2. *Could this man see his friends or talk to them?*
3. *How did Jesus feel when He saw this man?*
4. *What did Jesus do for him?*
5. *Do you think this man loved Jesus for being so kind to him?*

Parental Note: To illustrate this chapter, you might have your child close his/her eyes for one minute. Ask him/her how it felt and how this man must have felt when Jesus healed him.

CHAPTER 37

Jesus loved to tell the people around Him stories to teach them things. One day, He told them a story about a man who had many good things to eat and drink. This man built great big barns in which to keep all this food for himself.

When he had put all of it away, he said to himself, "You have plenty of good things laid up for many years. Take life easy; eat, drink, and be merry."

But as soon as the man said that, God spoke to him and told him, "You fool! This very night your life will be demanded from you." Then all the things that he had saved for himself would not do him any good. Instead, someone else would get it all.

Jesus told that story to teach us not to be like that man, because all the man cared about was to get rich and do what would please himself. Instead, we should always care about others and do what will make God happy.

QUESTIONS—CHAPTER 37

1. *Why did Jesus like to tell stories?*
2. *What did the man in this story have?*
3. *What did the man put in his barns?*
4. *When he had put everything away in the barns, what did he say to himself?*
5. *But what did God say to him?*
6. *Would all the things he had saved for himself do him any good?*
7. *Who should we try to make happy?*

Thought Question: Do the things we own make us safe?

Parental Note: Selfishness is a very real problem in our society. Underline this chapter by pointing out a recent family incident. Perhaps one of the children wouldn't share his/her toys.

CHAPTER 38

We learn all about Jesus and God, His Father, in the Bible. The Bible is what God wants us to know and learn about Him. One thing God wants us to know is that He loves us very much.

If we love Him and always obey Him, He will take good care of us and make sure we have clothes to wear and food to eat.

God gave the birds food to eat. He cares about the birds, and did you know that even if one tiny little bird falls out of its nest, God knows about it? But God cares a lot more about you and me and those who love Him than He does about the birds. He cares and knows so much about you that He even knows how many hairs are on your head!

So, if we love and obey God, we don't ever need to be afraid. God will never forget us, and He will always watch over us.

QUESTIONS—CHAPTER 38

1. *Who does the Bible tell us about?*
2. *Does God care about the birds?*
3. *But who does God care more about?*
4. *If we love and obey Jesus, what will God always do?*

Thought Question: Does God give us everything we want?

Can you count how many hairs this boy has on his head? God can. He knows how many you have, too. He cares about every one of them. He cares about every bit of you.

CHAPTER 39

Elijah was a prophet. A prophet was a man who would tell people what God wanted them to do, very much like a preacher.

In Elijah's country, there was a very bad king named Ahab, who was making the people of his country do very bad things. He made them worship idols instead of God.

Elijah went to see Ahab and told him God was very angry with him. As a punishment, he said, "There will be neither dew nor rain in the next few years except at my word."

And it didn't rain. Ahab began to worry and sent for Elijah. But no one could find Elijah because God had told him to go hide by a stream named Cherith. There Elijah had water and each day God sent big birds, called ravens, to bring him bread and meat.

God always takes care of us and provides just what we need.

QUESTIONS—CHAPTER 39

1. What was the name of the prophet?
2. What was Ahab making the people do?
3. What did Elijah tell Ahab?
4. What happened?
5. Where did Elijah go?
6. Who fed Elijah?
7. Who sent the ravens?

Thought Question: Give some examples of how God has taken care of you.

Can you see how hard it would have been for Elijah to survive in the desert country if God hadn't sent him water and food?

CHAPTER 40

One day, Jesus told a parable to some people who had gathered around Him. A parable is a story that is told in order to teach something very important. Sometimes it is much easier to learn that way.

This parable was about a man who went out into his field to plant some wheat. Bread is made out of wheat flour. Wheat grows up like tall grass and is harvested, and the little kernels of wheat are collected to grind into flour. To plant wheat a man takes some of these wheat kernels, before they are ground up, and plants them in the field. So the man in this parable took some wheat into his hand and scattered it on the ground as he walked along. But some wheat fell outside the field and the birds flew down and ate it up.

And some of the wheat fell in the wrong place—a place where there were lots of rocks and no soil so that the wheat could not form roots and grow up. The birds saw the wheat on the rocks and flew down to eat it up. So, no wheat grew up there.

Some of the wheat fell where there were lots of weeds and thorny bushes. The weeds and bushes would not give the wheat any room to grow so that no wheat grew up there.

But the rest of the wheat fell in the right place where the ground was soft and ready for it to come. The rain came down and the sun shone so that the wheat formed roots that went deep into the ground and the wheat grew tall. Soon it was harvested and the man had much more wheat than he had started with.

This same thing happens when I am teaching children what Jesus wants them to know. Some children do not listen to what I have to say, and then it is just as if some little bird came and took away every word I spoke, because the children do not remember them.

But some children do remember and try to obey what Jesus says. They are like the wheat that fell on the good ground and grew up to bear more wheat for the man who planted it.

QUESTIONS—CHAPTER 40

1. *What is a parable?*
2. *What was this man planting in his field?*
3. *Could the wheat that fell in the wrong place grow up?*
4. *What flew down and ate it up?*

What does this man have in his basket? What is he doing?

5. *Did the wheat that fell in the right place grow up and produce more wheat?*

6. *When children listen to what Jesus says and obey Him, then it is like the wheat*

that fell where?

Thought Question: What kind of soil are you?

CHAPTER 41

I was in my garden planting seeds today. Some were big seeds but some were very small. They will sprout in a few days and soon I will have pretty flowers.

Jesus told the people around Him about the mustard seed. It is a very small seed. It is about the size of a pin head. If you held one in your hand, you would hardly be able to see it. But if you planted it in the ground, it would sprout and grow into a tree big enough for birds to sit on its branches.

When little children first begin to love Jesus, their love is like a little mustard seed before it is planted in the ground, it is so small. But if the children keep on obeying Jesus and learn all they can about Him and talk to Him, their love will get bigger and bigger, like the mustard seed when it grows up to be a tree.

QUESTIONS—CHAPTER 41

1. *What kind of seed did Jesus tell the people about?*
2. *How big is the mustard seed?*
3. *When it is planted, what does it grow up to be?*
4. *When children first begin to love Jesus, what is their love like?*

Thought Question: Is bigger always better?

Have you ever seen a mustard seed? This shows how small it is. But when you plant it in the ground, it grows into a big tree.

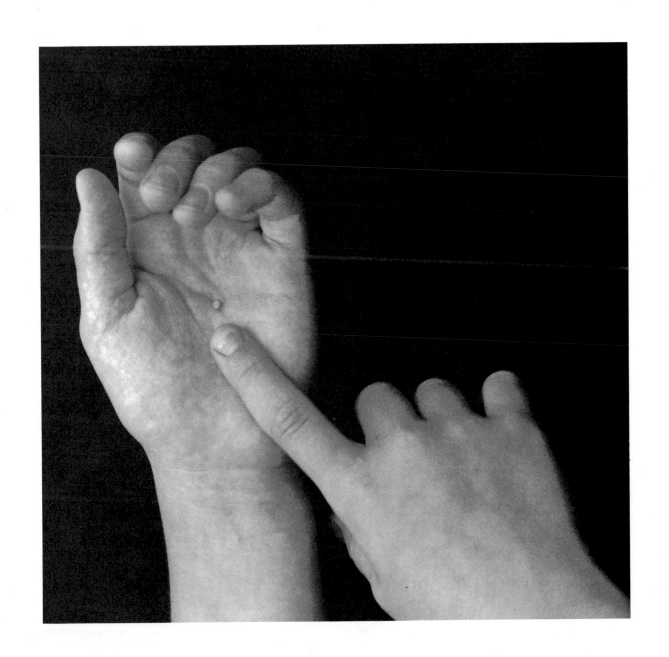

CHAPTER 42

I like to make bread. It makes the whole house smell good when it is baking in the oven, and then it tastes so good when I slice it while it is still hot and spread butter on it.

Jesus told a story about a woman making bread. First she takes some wheat flour, adds some water and salt, and begins to work it with her hands to make dough.

But then she takes something called yeast and adds some of the yeast to the dough. She works it some more with her hands—that is called kneading the dough. She kneads the dough so that the yeast will be mixed all through the dough. Then she sets the dough aside and covers it up and leaves it for several hours. The yeast makes the dough better than it was before, so that when it is put into the hot oven and baked, it makes nicer bread.

When little children love Jesus and obey Him, that makes them better children than they were before. If they love Him, they try very hard to do what pleases Him.

QUESTIONS—CHAPTER 42

1. *What was the woman in the story making?*
2. *After she had mixed the flour, salt, and water, what else did she add?*
3. *What does the yeast do?*
4. *When children love Jesus, does that make them better children than they were before?*
5. *What do they try to do?*

Have you ever helped to make bread? What do you think makes bread so fluffy and tasty?

MEMORY VERSE—Matthew 6:33 "But seek first his kingdom and his righteousness, and all these things will be given to you as well."

Jesus told the people a story about a man who wanted to buy some pearls. Pearls are beautiful little round white stones. Sometimes we see pearls in rings or bracelets or necklaces. Where do you think pearls come from? They come from under the water, way down under the ocean.

Trained divers dive down into the ocean and find oysters on the ocean floor; they bring these oysters up on the land, pry them open, and find pearls in them. Then they take out the pearls, and sell them to get money for them.

Once there was a man who wanted to buy some pearls. He did not want to dive down under the water to find them for himself, but he wanted to buy them from the divers who had found them already. So he went to these men and asked them to show him all the pearls they had to sell.

At last one of the men showed him a very beautiful pearl. It was larger and prettier than any pearl he had ever seen before, but it would cost more money than he had to buy it. So he told the man to keep that pearl until he came back again. Then he went away and sold everything he had, so he could get enough money to buy that pearl.

Perhaps he had horses, and cows, and sheep, and land; but he sold them all to get money for them to buy the pearl from the man. Then he was very happy, because he had the thing that he wanted more than anything else in this world.

What should we want more than anything else in this world? Not a pearl, for that will not make us happy. I will tell you.

We should want to please God and ask Him to come into our heart to live so that we are His children. We should obey Him, learn about Him and talk to Him. And when we do wrong, we should ask Him to forgive us.

We should want this as much as the man wanted the beautiful pearl.

QUESTIONS—CHAPTER 43

1. *What is a pearl?*
2. *Where do pearls come from?*
3. *What did the man in the story want?*
4. *Did he have enough money to buy the beautiful pearl?*
5. *What did he do to get enough money to buy it?*

6. *How did he feel when he got the pearl?*
7. *Did he want it more than anything else?*
8. *Should we want to please God that much?*

Thought Question: What do you want more than anything else?

Do you see the pearl that is so much bigger and prettier than the others? We should want to please God as much as the man in the story wanted the beautiful pearl like this one.

CHAPTER 44

I have told you what a fishing net is. It is made of rope; men catch fish with it. Let me tell you how they do this. They put the net in a boat and row the boat out on the water. Then they throw the net into the water, and the fish that are swimming there are caught in the net.

Then the men pull up the net and take the fish out of it. But the fish are not all alike. Some are good: these the men put in a basket to keep; and some of them are bad: these they throw away.

Jesus said that all the men and women and little children in the world are either good or bad, like the fish that are caught in the net. But one day God will send His angels to take to heaven those men and women and children who have Jesus as their Savior, and who show it by doing good. But the bad men, women, and children will be sent away to the place where they are to be punished for their sins.

QUESTIONS—CHAPTER 44

1. *What are fishing nets used for?*
2. *Are all the fish alike?*
3. *Who did Jesus say were like the fish in the net?*
4. *One day what will happen to good men and women and children?*
5. *What will happen to bad men and women and children on that day?*

These fishing nets are like the ones in the story. The fishermen have hung them in the sun to dry.

One day a man came to Jesus and told Him that he wanted to stay with Him and live with Him all the time. But Jesus told the man that He had no home to live in.

Jesus said that the little birds had homes—they had their nests up in the trees. And the wild animals had homes—they had caves and holes in the ground where they could go. But when Jesus was tired He had no place where He could go to lie down to rest.

It was because He didn't have anything that Jesus had no home. He was poorer even than the birds and the animals. But Jesus was not always poor. He used to live in heaven—He was not poor there. He had everything to make Him happy.

Why, then, did He come to this world where He would be poor, and have trouble? It was because He loved us, and He wanted to make us God's children, so that we, too, might go to heaven after we die. If Jesus loved us so much to come from heaven for us, we ought to love Him and ask Him to come into our hearts to live.

QUESTIONS—CHAPTER 45

1. *What did the man who came to Jesus tell Him that he wanted to do?*
2. *What did Jesus tell the man?*
3. *What did Jesus say about the birds and the animals?*
4. *What was the reason Jesus had no home?*
5. *Was Jesus always poor?*
6. *Why did He come to this world to be poor and have trouble?*
7. *What should we do?*

Thought Question: If your friends made fun of you and your family made you leave home, would you still serve Jesus?

Parental Note: See parental note, chapter 13.

A man wanted to come and live with Jesus. Jesus told him he couldn't, because Jesus had no home. Why didn't He have a home?

CHAPTER 46

Jesus got into a boat with His disciples to go across the lake. While they were sailing across the lake, He lay down and went to sleep. He was tired.

Pretty soon a storm arose that made the waves very high and rough. The little boat was being tossed around on the water, and water was getting into the boat. The disciples were scared. They were afraid that the boat would sink.

They woke Jesus up and said, "Lord, save us, we're going to drown!"

Jesus asked the disciples why they were afraid of the wind and the waves while He was there to keep them safe. Then Jesus stood up in the boat and told the wind not to blow and the waves to be calm.

Do you know what? The wind and waves obeyed Him. The wind quit blowing and the waves calmed.

The disciples were amazed when they saw this happen. They said to each other, "Even the winds and the waves obey Him!"

QUESTIONS—CHAPTER 46

1. *What did Jesus and His disciples get into to go to the other side of the lake?*
2. *What did Jesus do?*
3. *What did the storm do?*
4. *How did the disciples feel? What did they do?*
5. *What did they say to Jesus?*
6. *Should they have been afraid while He was with them?*

Thought Question: If you had been in the boat that day what would you have done?

This famous painting of the storm described in the story was made by the artist Rembrandt more than 300 years ago. Doesn't Jesus look calm?

CHAPTER 47

Remember I told you about the good angels that live in heaven? But also there are some very bad angels. They do not live in heaven; no one bad or wicked lives in heaven. We call these bad angels demons; that is their name.

These demons do not have bodies like ours with hands and feet. We cannot see these demons and they can go into places where we cannot go. Sometimes demons go into people and make the people act very, very bad. But if Jesus lives in our hearts and we obey Him, then the demons cannot come into us.

When Jesus got out of the boat and walked on the shore, a man came to Him who had demons in him. The demons made this man very angry and mean so that he acted like a wild animal. All the people were afraid of him and stayed very far away from him.

The man's friends had tried to keep him at home; they had put chains around his hands and feet to keep him home, but he broke the chains and went to roam around in the mountains.

There were caves in these mountains. Caves are hollow places dug out of the ground that are like big, dark rooms. Some caves had been dug out of these mountains in which to bury dead people. Sometimes wild animals live in the caves. This poor man with the demons in him lived in these caves.

At night he could not sleep, so he would scream all night long, and sometimes he would pick up sharp rocks and cut himself on purpose. The demons in him made him do these awful things.

The poor man could do nothing to make the demons go away. But Jesus could make them leave. So now Jesus spoke to the demons and told them to come out of the man. Immediately they came out of him.

Close by there was a big herd of pigs that were eating. When the demons came out of the man, they went into the pigs. The demons made the pigs run into the lake and they all drowned in the water.

But the man was different. He was not mean and angry; instead he was quiet and well like other people because Jesus had made the demons leave him. He thanked Jesus and wanted to follow Him to stay with Him all the time. But Jesus told him to go home and tell his friends how he had been made well.

QUESTIONS—CHAPTER 47

1. *What are the bad angels called?*
2. *Do the demons have hands and feet as we do?*
3. *Can we see them?*
4. *If Jesus lives in our hearts, can demons come into us?*
5. *When Jesus was walking on the shore,* *who came to Him?*
6. *What had the demons made this man act like?*
7. *What did Jesus make the demons do?*
8. *Where did the demons go?*
9. *Was the man well after that?*
10. *What did Jesus tell him to do?*

Parental Note: The fact of demons should not scare a child. The emphasis should be put on Jesus' power and His love and care for us.

Jesus and His disciples again went to Capernaum. A big crowd was following Him. Some of the people were very close to Him and pushing against Him.

In the crowd there was a woman who had been sick for a long, long time. She had gone to see many doctors, hoping they could make her well. She had spent all her money but they could not cure her. And now she was in the crowd that was following Jesus.

As soon as she saw Him, she said to herself, "If only I could get close enough behind Him and touch His clothes, I am sure I would be well." So she crept up quietly behind Jesus, reached out, and touched Him. Immediately, she knew that she was well.

Then Jesus stopped and looked around. He asked, "Who touched Me?" The disciples had not seen the woman do it, and with so many people crowded around, they wondered why Jesus asked who had touched Him. But Jesus said, "Someone touched me; I know that power has gone out from me."

When the woman saw that Jesus knew she had touched Him and that she could not hide, she was afraid. She came to Jesus and knelt in front of Him. She told Him that it was she who had touched Him and had been made well.

Jesus spoke to her very kindly and called her "daughter." He said, "Daughter, your faith has healed you. Go in peace."

QUESTIONS—CHAPTER 48

1. *When Jesus was in Capernaum, who was following Him?*
2. *What had the woman spent all her money doing?*
3. *Did the doctors cure her?*
4. *What did she say to herself when she saw Jesus?*
5. *What happened when she touched Him?*
6. *Did Jesus know what she had done?*
7. *Was she afraid?*
8. *Was Jesus kind to her? What did He call her?*
9. *What did He tell her?*

Thought Question: If you are being pushed and shoved in a crowd do you get angry and scared? How did Jesus act?

Jesus was walking down a crowded street like this one when the sick woman touched Him. Why did she do that?

CHAPTER 49

A man came to Jesus who was very upset because his little girl was sick and he was afraid she was going to die. The man said, "Please come and put your hands on her so that she will be healed and live."

So Jesus went with the man, but as they were approaching the house, someone came to them and told the man, "Your daughter is dead; why bother the Teacher any more?" But Jesus told the man, "Don't be afraid; just believe."

When they went inside the house, the people were crying; they were very sad that the little girl was dead. Jesus told them all to go out of the house, but He took three of His disciples and the little girl's parents into the room where she lay.

Jesus went to the side of her bed, held her hand, and said, "Little girl, I say to you, get up!" As soon as He said that, the little girl opened her eyes, sat up, and began to walk. She was twelve years old and alive again!

Jesus told her parents to get her something to eat. They were so happy because their little girl was alive and would live with them and love them just as before.

QUESTIONS—CHAPTER 49

1. *Why was the man who came to Jesus so upset?*
2. *What did he ask Jesus to do?*
3. *When they were approaching the man's house, what did someone tell them?*
4. *What did Jesus tell the man?*
5. *When Jesus went beside the little girl's bed, what did He say to her?*
6. *What happened to the little girl?*
7. *How did her parents feel when they saw she was alive?*

Thought Question: When you are sad, is it okay to cry?

Who is lying on the bed in this picture? Can you tell which of these men is Jesus? What is He doing?

CHAPTER 50

As Jesus was leaving that place, two blind men followed Him. They could not see Him, but someone had told them that Jesus was there. Perhaps they had heard how He brought the little girl to life again, and they thought He could make their eyes well.

So the blind men followed Jesus, and called after Him, saying, "Have mercy on us, Son of David." Jesus stopped and asked them, "Do you believe that I am able to do this?" They said, "Yes, Lord." "According to your faith will it be done to you," He said. Then He put out His hand and touched their eyes. By only touching them, He made their eyes well.

Then the men went away and told all the people who lived in that country how Jesus had cured them in one moment and made them able to see.

QUESTIONS—CHAPTER 50

1. *As Jesus was leaving, who followed Him?*
2. *What did the blind men want Him to do?*
3. *What did Jesus ask the blind men?*
4. *How did He make their eyes well?*
5. *What did the blind men do after they were made well?*

Thought Question: If you had been one of those blind men, would you have gone to Jesus?

A blind person cannot see all the beautiful things God has made, like the sun and the sky. Close your eyes and imagine what it would be like.

CHAPTER 51

Some people brought to Jesus a man who could not talk. He had been able to talk once, like you and me, but now a demon had gone into him that would not allow him to talk.

None of the man's friends could make the demon leave; but Jesus made the demon leave, and then the man was able to speak.

The people who saw Jesus make the demon leave the man were surprised. They said they had never seen such a wonderful thing done before.

QUESTIONS—CHAPTER 51

1. *Who was brought to Jesus?*
2. *What was it that made him unable to talk?*
3. *Could the man's friends make the demon leave?*
4. *But what did Jesus do?*
5. *Could the man talk after that?*

Thought Question: Does Jesus still have power over demons?

The man who could not talk must really have loved Jesus for healing him, don't you think? Jesus can help you, too, if you believe in Him.

CHAPTER 52

After this, Jesus went into other towns to teach the people who lived there. But He could not teach all the people in that country by Himself: there were too many of them. So He sent out His twelve disciples to teach the people who lived in the cities where He Himself could not go.

The twelve disciples went to those towns and taught the people about Jesus. They told the people how He had come down from heaven to take away their sins and to make them God's children. Jesus enabled the disciples to make sick people well and dead people alive, just as Jesus did Himself. Jesus let the disciples do these wonderful things so that the people might listen to what they said and might believe that God had sent them.

After the apostles had taught the people, they came back to Jesus. They told Him where they had been and what they had done.

QUESTIONS—CHAPTER 52

1. *Did Jesus go into other towns to teach the people?*
2. *Why could He not teach all the people in that country by Himself?*
3. *Whom did He send to teach the people in the towns where He could not go?*
4. *What did He enable the disciples to do while they were teaching the people there?*
5. *Could they have done this without Jesus' help?*

Thought Question: Can you also go out and tell people about Jesus like the apostles did?

Jesus went into other towns to teach the people who lived there. Who are the other men in this picture? What is Jesus telling them to do?

CHAPTER 53

Jesus and His disciples wanted to be alone, so they got into a boat and went to the other side of the lake. But when the people saw where Jesus was going, they followed Him. It was a very big crowd of people.

Jesus was very kind to them; He taught them many things about God and heaven. The people that were sick, He made well.

When it started getting dark, the disciples went to Jesus and said, "This is a remote place and it is already very late. Send the people away so they can go to the surrounding countryside and villages and buy themselves something to eat." Jesus didn't want to send the people away, so He told the disciples, "You give them something to eat."

The disciples told Jesus, "That would take eight months of a man's wages! Are we to go and spend that much on bread and give it to them to eat?" Jesus asked them, "How many loaves do you have?" They told Him they had only five loaves of bread and two small fish.

Then Jesus told the disciples to have all the people sit down on the grass in rows. He held the loaves of bread and the fish in His hands, prayed, and thanked God for the food. He then broke the bread and fish into pieces and gave them to the disciples to pass out to the people.

As they were giving out the pieces of fish, they didn't run out of food, because as they gave out a piece of fish or bread another piece would come. The pieces kept on coming until all the men, women, and children who had followed Jesus had had all they wanted to eat.

After they were finished, Jesus told the disciples to pick up the pieces of fish and bread that were left over. He didn't want any food wasted. They picked up all the food that was left and found that they had twelve baskets of food left over! This was a lot more food than they had had when they began to feed the people.

It was Jesus who made the bread and fish keep coming until all the people had enough to eat. This was a miracle. We cannot do miracles, but Jesus can, because He is the Son of God and He can do the same things that God can do.

QUESTIONS—CHAPTER 53

1. *Where did Jesus and His disciples go?*
2. *Who followed Him there?*

3. *Was Jesus kind to the crowd that followed Him?*
4. *Why did the disciples want to send the people home?*
5. *What did Jesus tell the disciples to do?*
6. *Did they think they had enough food to feed the people?*
7. *How many loaves of bread and fish did they have?*
8. *Whom did Jesus thank for the food?*
9. *While the disciples were giving out the pieces of bread and fish to the people, what happened?*
10. *Did everyone get as much as they wanted to eat?*
11. *How many baskets full of food were left over?*
12. *Who was it that made the pieces of bread and fish keep on coming until the people had enough to eat?*
13. *What was this called?*
14. *Why could Jesus do miracles?*

Thought Question: When the disciples looked at the crowds then at the small amount of food what did they see? What did Jesus see instead?

This boy has five loaves of bread and two fishes. Jesus fed hundreds of people with this much food. We call this a miracle.

CHAPTER 54

After all the people had eaten as much as they wanted, Jesus sent them home. He told the disciples to get into a boat and sail to the other side of the lake. Jesus wanted to be alone, so He stayed by Himself on the beach. When the disciples left, He went up on a mountainside to pray. He knelt down on the ground and prayed to God.

During the night Jesus came back down from the mountainside to the beach. He saw the disciples out in the middle of the lake struggling with their boat because the wind was blowing hard against them. The waves were high and rough.

So Jesus went out to them, walking on the water. He walked on the water as if it were dry land! When the disciples saw Him coming toward them walking on the water, they were afraid. They did not know who or what it was.

But Jesus called out to them and told them, "Take courage! It is I. Don't be afraid." One of the disciples named Peter asked Jesus if he could come out to meet Jesus on the water. Jesus answered yes. So Peter got out of the boat and began to walk on the water towards Jesus.

But when he heard the loud wind and saw the rough waves all around him, he got scared and began to sink. He called out to Jesus and said, "Lord, save me or I will drown."

Jesus reached out His hand and held Peter up so that he would not sink into the water. Jesus asked Peter why he was afraid while he was with Him. Jesus would take care of him and keep him safe.

Then Jesus and Peter got into the boat with the other disciples. When they got into the boat, the wind and waves calmed down and they were able to cross the lake.

They got out of the boat and walked on the beach. Soon the people heard that Jesus was there, and they began to bring their sick friends to Him to be made well.

Wherever He went, the people brought sick people to Him, even if they had to carry the persons on their beds and lay them in the street so that they might only touch Jesus' clothes as He walked by. Everyone who touched Him was made whole.

QUESTIONS—CHAPTER 54

1. *After all the people had gone, what did Jesus go up on the mountainside to do?*
2. *When He came down, where did He see the disciples?*
3. *How did Jesus get to them?*
4. *When the disciples saw Him, were they afraid?*
5. *What did Peter ask Jesus?*
6. *What happened to Peter as he was walking on the water?*
7. *How did Jesus save him?*
8. *What did Jesus ask Peter?*
9. *When they got into the boat, what happened?*
10. *When Jesus walked on the beach, who did the people bring to Him?*
11. *Did Jesus make all the people whole again?*

Thought Question: If you had been in the boat that night would you have gotten out like Peter did?

CHAPTER 55

Then Jesus came to a town named Bethsaida, and some people brought a blind man to Him. They begged Jesus to make the blind man well so that he could see. Jesus felt sorry for the man, took him by the hand, and led him out of town. Jesus put His hands on the blind man's eyes. Then He asked him, "Do you see anything?"

The blind man said, "I see people; they look like trees walking around."

So Jesus put His hands on the blind man's eyes again. After that his eyes were well, and he could see everything clearly.

QUESTIONS—CHAPTER 55

1. *When Jesus came to Bethsaida, who was brought to Him?*
2. *What did Jesus do to the blind man's eyes to make them well?*
3. *Was the man able to see clearly at first?*
4. *What did he say the men looked like who were passing by?*
5. *What did Jesus do to his eyes again?*
6. *Was the man able to see everything clearly after that?*

Thought Question: Why do you think Jesus didn't heal the man's eyes on the first touch?

After Jesus touched the blind man's eyes the second time, he could see all the beautiful things God made, like these butterflies.

CHAPTER 56

Jesus took three of His disciples with Him, and He went up on a lonely mountain to pray. While He was praying, His face was changed so that it looked bright and shining, like the sun. And His clothes looked as white as snow.

All of a sudden two men joined them there. They were Moses and Elijah, two great prophets who had lived a long time ago and now lived in heaven. They did not look like other men: they looked more beautiful.

We do not know where heaven is. But Moses and Elijah live there and now they had come back to this world where we live, and where they used to live. They had come back for only a little while to talk with Jesus.

Soon a bright cloud came onto the mountain; it covered the three disciples, and they heard a voice speaking out of the cloud. It was God's voice. It said, "This is My Son, Whom I love. Listen to Him."

When the disciples heard God's voice, they were afraid. They knelt down and put their faces to the ground. But Jesus came and put His hand on them and told them to stand up and not be afraid.

They stood up and looked around, but the two men were not there now: they had gone back to heaven.

QUESTIONS—CHAPTER 56

1. *How many disciples went with Jesus to the mountaintop?*
2. *What happened while Jesus was praying?*
3. *Who were the two men who came to talk to Jesus?*
4. *Where do Moses and Elijah live?*
5. *What covered the mountain and the disciples?*
6. *Whose voice spoke out of the cloud?*
7. *What did God's voice say?*
8. *How did the disciples feel when they heard God's voice?*
9. *When the disciples got up from the ground, were the two men there?*
10. *Where had they gone?*

Thought Question: How does God speak to us today?

Jesus went up on a lonely mountain to pray. How many disciples went with Him? What did they see?

CHAPTER 57

MEMORY VERSE—Proverbs 1:10 My son, if sinners entice you, do not give in to them.

Even though Jesus had been very kind to the people in that country, they did not love Him. Do you know why they didn't love Him? Because He told them about their sins. Remember I told you what sins are—they are all the bad things we do, like disobeying our parents or telling something that isn't true. Jesus told these people they must stop sinning. If they did not stop, God would punish them.

But the people did not want to stop; they enjoyed doing the bad things and they did not want to be told about their sins. They got angry at Jesus for telling them about their sins and wanted to kill Him so that He wouldn't talk any more.

Jesus knew what they were going to do. He told His disciples that one day He would be killed. But He would come alive again and come out of the grave.

QUESTIONS—CHAPTER 57

1. *Had Jesus been very kind to the people in that country?*
2. *Did the people love Him?*
3. *Why?*
4. *What is sin?*
5. *What did the people want to do to Jesus for telling them about their sins?*
6. *Did Jesus know that they wanted to kill Him?*

Thought Question: Do you enjoy doing things you know you shouldn't?

This picture shows the people threatening to kill Jesus, even though He loved them. Why did they want to kill Him?

CHAPTER 58

One day when the disciples were walking along together they began to argue with each other. Each one of them thought that the others should obey him; this made them argue.

When they came into the house, Jesus asked them what they had been arguing about. They were ashamed and did not want to tell Him; they did not think that He had heard them. But He knows everything we say, and He knew what they had said when they were arguing with one another.

Then Jesus told the disciples that they should not want other persons to obey them, but they must be willing to obey what other persons said. Jesus is not happy with us when we are proud and when we think we are better than other people. He is happy with us when we are humble and think of other people first instead of ourselves.

QUESTIONS—CHAPTER 58

1. *What did the disciples do while they were walking together one day?*
2. *What made them argue?*
3. *Did they think that Jesus had heard what they said?*
4. *Does Jesus know everything we say?*
5. *When He asked the disciples why they had been arguing, how did they feel?*
6. *What did He say?*
7. *Is Jesus pleased with us when we are proud, and when we think that we are better than other people?*
8. *Does he tell us to think of other people first?*

Thought Question: Do you like to be first?

These two children are playing nicely together and sharing. That makes Jesus happy.

CHAPTER 59

Sometimes little children want to do wrong; sometimes they like that more than they like to do right. But Jesus says we must not do what is wrong: and if we are doing wrong, we must stop doing it, no matter how hard it is to stop. If we ask Him to help us to stop, He will.

If we know that we are doing wrong and will not stop, then we will be punished. We should obey God and do what is right; that makes God happy with us.

Perhaps someone is unkind to you or hurts you and you get very angry with him. Jesus said, "If he sins against you seven times in a day, and seven times comes back to you and says 'I repent,' forgive him." And if he is unkind to us many times, but later says he is sorry, we must forgive him every time, no matter how often it may be.

QUESTIONS—CHAPTER 59

1. *Do little children sometimes like to do wrong more than they like to do right?*
2. *If we go on doing wrong and will not stop, what will happen to us?*
3. *What should we do?*
4. *If any person is unkind to us and later says he is sorry for it, what must we do?*
5. *Should we forgive him every time he says he is sorry, no matter how often it is?*

Thought Question: Is it easy to forgive someone who has hurt you?

If someone you know is unkind to you, then says he's sorry, what does Jesus say you must do?

CHAPTER 60

Remember I told you that Jesus loved to tell stories called parables to teach the people something important? Well, one day Jesus told His disciples a parable about a king. This king had a man who worked for him who had borrowed some money from the king. Now the king wanted the money back but the man did not have any money with which to pay the king.

In that country, if you needed money and you had no other way of getting some, you could sell yourself, your wife, and your children to be slaves for someone. This is what the king told the man he must do to get the money to pay him back. This made the man very sad.

He came to the king, knelt on the ground in front of the king, and begged him to wait just a little while longer so that he could find some other way to get the money, rather than sell his family. He promised the king that as soon as he got the money, he would repay him.

When the king saw how upset the man was, he felt sorry for him and told him that he should not sell his family to get the money. In fact, the king would forget all about the money the man owed him and the man would never have to pay him back. This made the man so happy, and he thanked the king for being so kind to him.

When the man left the king's palace, he met a man who owed him some money and he told this man to pay him. This poor man said he couldn't but promised to as soon as he could.

The man who worked for the king got very mad and grabbed the man around the throat and demanded to be paid the money. He could not wait. Because the poor man could not pay him immediately, the man who worked for the king had him thrown into prison.

Soon the king heard about this, and he got very angry. He sent for the man who worked for him and said, "You are a wicked man; I forgave you when you couldn't pay me, so you should forgive the poor man who couldn't pay you." Then the king sent the man away to be punished.

Jesus told this story to teach us that we must forgive other people when they have said or done something unkind to us. Jesus said, "This is how My Heavenly Father will treat you unless you forgive your brother from your heart."

QUESTIONS—CHAPTER 60

1. *When the man could not pay the money, what did the king say must be done to him and his wife and his children?*
2. *When the man heard this, what did he kneel down and ask the king to do?*
3. *What did the king do?*
4. *When the servant went out of the king's house, whom did he meet?*
5. *Was the man able to pay him the money right away?*
6. *When the man asked the king's servant to wait until he could get some money to pay him with, was he willing to wait?*
7. *Where did he send the man?*
8. *How did the king feel when he heard how cruel the man who worked for him had been?*
9. *What does this story teach us?*

CHAPTER 61

One day while Jesus and His disciples were walking together, they came close to a small town. Many people lived in this town. Jesus sent some of His disciples into town to ask the people if they would let Him stop there to rest and eat.

But the people in the town were very unfriendly and unkind to Jesus. They told Him that He could not stop. Two of the disciples, James and John, got very mad at the people and wanted to punish them. They asked Jesus if they could bring down fire from heaven to burn up the houses and all the people.

Jesus was sad that the people in the town did not want Him to stop, but He was displeased with James and John for wanting to do such a mean thing. Jesus told James and John, "The Son of Man did not come to destroy men's lives, but to save them."

He did not punish the people who were so unfriendly and unkind, but went on to another town to rest and eat.

QUESTIONS—CHAPTER 61

1. *What did Jesus send some of His disciples into the town to ask the people?*
2. *What did the people say to Jesus' disciples?*
3. *How did James and John feel?*
4. *What did they want to do?*
5. *Was Jesus displeased that James and John wanted to do this?*
6. *What did Jesus say that he had come to this world for?*
7. *Instead of punishing the people, what did He do?*

Thought Question: Do you sometimes like to get back at someone who's been mean to you, as James and John wanted to do?

Here is a town like the one in the story. Were the town people friendly to Jesus? Did Jesus stay in the town to rest and eat?

CHAPTER 62

Jesus told the people another story. He told them about a man traveling alone down a dangerous road. It was dangerous because there were many places along the road where bad men, called robbers, could hide and then run out to beat up a traveler and take his money.

The man in Jesus' story was walking along when all of a sudden robbers jumped out of their hiding place and beat up this poor man. They took everything that he had—food, clothes, and money. Then they left him beside the road to die.

After a while another man came down the road. He was a priest in the temple who would tell people to be kind to each other. But, unfortunately, he was not kind himself, and so he passed the poor man who had been so badly beaten by the robbers. He crossed over to the other side of the road, pretended not to see the man, and went away.

Soon another man came down the road, but he didn't help the poor man either. He kept on walking just as the priest had done and left the man on the ground.

But after these men had passed by without helping the poor man, someone else came by. He was called a Samaritan, and he was riding on a donkey. As soon as he saw the man lying beside the road, he stopped and got down to help him.

The Samaritan was very kind and gentle. He lifted the poor man carefully and put him on the donkey; then he walked very carefully and slowly beside the donkey with his arm around the wounded man so he would not fall off. The Samaritan took the man to a nearby house and stayed up all night to take care of him.

The next day when the Samaritan had to go away, he gave some money to the man who owned the house and asked him to take care of the sick man until he got well.

Jesus told this story to teach us to be like the Good Samaritan man. We should be kind to everyone we meet but especially to those who need our help. We should always be helpful whenever we can be, even when it is a lot of trouble for us.

QUESTIONS—CHAPTER 62

1. Who came out and beat up the man in the story and took everything that he had?
2. After this happened, who first came down the road?
3. What did he tell people to do?
4. Was he good and kind himself?
5. Instead of helping the wounded man, what did he do?
6. When another man came by, what did he do?
7. What did Jesus want to teach us by telling this story?
8. Should we always be kind to everyone we meet, especially when they need our help?

Thought Question: Which man in this story are you like? Can you think of a time you helped someone who needed you?

Parental Note: Our society is very selfish; we "don't want to get involved." But this is contrary to the teaching of Jesus. Begin to instill in your child thoughtfulness and unselfishness.

CHAPTER 63

Jesus went to visit some friends of His who lived in a town called Bethany. His friends were named Mary and Martha; they were sisters. They also had a brother named Lazarus.

When Jesus came into their house, Mary stopped what she was doing to sit near Jesus to listen to what He was saying. Mary wanted to learn all about how her sins could be forgiven and how she would go to heaven when she died.

But Martha, her sister, thought Mary should be doing her work and asked Jesus to tell Mary to get busy. Jesus said, "Martha, Martha, you are worried and upset about many things, but only one thing is needed. Mary has chosen what is better." It was more important for Mary to learn what He had to say and the things He taught than to be busy doing other things.

QUESTIONS—CHAPTER 63

1. *What were the names of the two sisters?*
2. *When Jesus came into the house, what did Mary do?*
3. *Why did she want to listen to Jesus?*
4. *How did this make Martha feel?*
5. *What did Martha ask Jesus to tell Mary?*
6. *What did Jesus tell Martha?*

Thought Question: Is it easier for you to play with your toys or go to Sunday School?

Parental Note: Priorities are an important lesson, but perhaps more so for us as parents than for our children. What are our priorities? Our children should be one of those at the top of our list. Raising children is very hard work in our society. It is a huge responsibility, not to be taken lightly. In Mark 9:37, Jesus said, "Whoever welcomes one of these little children in my name welcomes me." So our work with our children is done as unto Jesus. In Mark 10:14, Jesus said, "Let the little children come to me, and do not hinder them, for the kingdom of God belongs to such as these." Let us not hinder our children by being too busy with other matters.

An artist named Alessandro Allori painted this picture in the sixteenth century. Who are the two ladies in the picture? When Jesus came to their house, what did they do?

CHAPTER 64

Jesus taught the people what they should say when they were praying to God. He said, "When you pray, say, 'Our Father in heaven, Hallowed be Your name. Your kingdom come. Your will be done on earth as it is in heaven. Give us today our daily bread. Forgive us our debts, as we also have forgiven our debtors. And lead us not into temptation, but deliver us from the evil one; for Yours is the kingdom and the power, and the glory forever. Amen.'"

This is called the Lord's Prayer, because the Lord Jesus teaches us to say it. But whenever we say this prayer, we must remember that we are speaking to God; and we must think of what we are saying.

Jesus not only teaches us to say the Lord's Prayer, but He tells us to pray to God for everything that we need. For God is our Father who lives in heaven, and He loves to give His children the things they pray for, and the things that are best for them.

QUESTIONS—CHAPTER 64

1. *What did Jesus teach the people?*
2. *What is the name of the prayer that Jesus taught them?*
3. *When we say this prayer, to whom are we speaking?*
4. *What should we pray to God for?*
5. *Does God love to give to His children the things they pray for?*

Thought Question: Can you think of something you prayed about and how God answered?

Parental Note: Prayer cannot be overemphasized. But we can't expect our children to learn to pray if we don't pray ourselves. Children's prayers are so precious as they learn to talk to Jesus. What a privilege to teach them how! Remind them that they can pray about anything: needs, wisdom, guidance, protection, friends, sick pets, sore fingers, help in finding a lost toy—everything!

This is part of a picture painted by Sir Joshua Reynolds about 200 years ago. In it, Samuel is praying to God. Do you remember to ask God for the things you need?

CHAPTER 65

As Jesus was going along the street, He saw a man who was blind, even when he was a little boy. Now the man had grown up, but he could not work and earn money because he could not see.

So, he would sit down in the street and beg the people who passed by to give him some of their money, so that he might buy food to eat and clothes to wear.

When Jesus saw the man, He was sorry for him. He stooped down, took some dirt from the ground, and put it on the blind man's eyes. Then He told him, "Go wash in the Pool of Siloam."

So the man went to the pool and washed his eyes and he could see! But it was not the dirt or the water in the pool that made his eyes well. It was Jesus who made them well, so that that man was able to see.

When the people who had known him before saw the blind man walking along like any other person who could see, they wondered and said, "Isn't this the same man who used to sit and beg?"

Some claimed that it was the man.

Others said, "No, he only looks like him." But the man himself said, "I am the man." Then they asked him, "How then were your eyes opened?" He told them, "The man they call Jesus made some mud and put it on my eyes. He told me to go to Siloam and wash. So I went and washed, and then I could see."

But the men who asked him were not happy with what he told them. These men were bad. They did not love Jesus and would not believe that He could make blind people well. So when the man said that it was Jesus who had made him well, they were angry with the man and would not talk to him or have anything to do with him.

Jesus heard how unkind they had been to the man. He found him and asked him, "Do you believe in the Son of Man?" "Who is He, Sir?" the man asked. "Tell me so that I may believe in Him." Jesus said, "You have now seen Him; in fact, He is the One speaking with you." Then the man said, "Lord, I believe," and he worshiped Him.

QUESTIONS—CHAPTER 65

1. *What was the matter with the man whom Jesus saw in the street begging?*
2. *What did Jesus put on the blind man's eyes?*
3. *Then what did Jesus tell him to do?*
4. *When the man had washed his eyes in the pool, what happened?*
5. *Who had made his eyes well?*
6. *How did the people treat the man when he told them that it was Jesus who cured him?*
7. *When Jesus told the man that it was God's Son who had made him well, what did the man do?*

Thought Question: Do you have some friends who don't think Jesus can help them?

CHAPTER 66

Remember I told you about Jesus' friends Mary and Martha, who had a brother named Lazarus? When Jesus had left their house, Lazarus got very sick. So Mary and Martha sent someone to tell Jesus, "Lord, the one You love is sick."

When Jesus heard this, He came back to their house because He loved them very much. But by the time Jesus got there, Lazarus was already dead and had been buried. The people who were with Mary and Martha were all crying because they were so sad that Lazarus was dead. When Martha heard that Jesus was coming, she went out to meet him, but Mary stayed at home.

"Lord," Martha said to Jesus, "if You had been here, my brother would not have died. But I know even now God will give You whatever You ask."

Jesus said to her, "Your brother will rise again. . . . I am the resurrection and the life. He who believes in Me will live, even though he dies."

Jesus asked them where they had buried Lazarus, so they took Him to the place. It was a cave with a big stone rolled over the front of it. Jesus then told the people to roll the stone out of the way. So they did.

Jesus said in a loud voice, "Lazarus, come out!" As soon as He said that, Lazarus came out! He was alive! Jesus had made Lazarus alive again by just saying those words. Jesus did this miracle so that people would honor God and Jesus.

Jesus told the people nearby to unfasten the cloth that had been tightly wrapped around Lazarus for burial so that Lazarus could walk. Then Lazarus went home with his sisters, Mary and Martha, and lived there just as he did before.

QUESTIONS—CHAPTER 66

1. *What was the name of Mary and Martha's brother?*
2. *When Lazarus got sick, did they send someone to tell Jesus?*
3. *What had already happened to Lazarus when Jesus arrived?*
4. *Where had they buried him?*
5. *When they had taken the stone out of the way, what did Jesus say?*
6. *What happened?*
7. *Who made Lazarus alive?*
8. *Why did Jesus do this miracle?*

Thought Question: If you had been at Lazarus' grave that day, how would you have felt?

Parental Note: Death is a matter to be discussed with children. It is more frightening to a child to be uncertain about such a subject than to learn about it. But here the emphasis always should be not on death but on the promise of a wonderful heavenly home with Jesus if we have asked Him into our hearts. No doubt a member of the family—perhaps a great-grandparent or grandparent—has died during your child's lifetime. I know that in our case, while there was sorrow and tears because of our loss, there was great joy knowing that loved one was in heaven with Jesus and we would see him again one day.

This is a graveyard in the Holy Land. See if you can find some crosses carved in one of the stones. They mark the doorway to one of the burial places.

CHAPTER 67

After this, many people came to listen to Jesus and to learn what He would teach them. Jesus told the people that if they loved Him, they would always obey Him, even if it was something they didn't want to do. He said, "If anyone would come after me, he must deny himself and take up his cross daily and follow me."

Let me try to explain to you what this means. Suppose one day you were playing outside with some other boys and girls, but one of the little boys got too rough and started to hurt one of your friends. Your friend was smaller than the others and could not play as well as they could, so the children made fun of him.

You didn't like them to make fun of him and hurt his feelings, so you protected him and made a special effort to be kind and play with him even though the other children now wouldn't play with you.

This is taking up your cross. It is doing something that is right even though it might cause you to lose some friends or to be hurt. You do it because Jesus would have done the same thing.

Or suppose someone gave you a brand new, crisp dollar bill and told you to go buy something you wanted. So you thought of a toy you had been wanting and your mother took you to the store to buy it. But as you were going into the store, you saw a friend of yours who never had money to buy toys. You stopped and thought about the nice toys you had at home that this little friend had admired. So you went over to him and gave him the new dollar bill and told him to go buy something he wanted. He smiled, thanked you, and hurried off to buy something he wanted. He was happy.

This is taking up the cross to put someone else first instead of always thinking about yourself and what you want.

And do you know what happens to you? This makes you happy because in your heart you know you have done the right thing and you have made Jesus happy.

QUESTIONS—CHAPTER 67

1. *What did Jesus say the people must do if they loved Him?*
2. *What did He call this?*
3. *If you do something right even if it may hurt you or cause you to lose friends, is this taking up the cross?*
4. *Is thinking of other people, rather than*

yourself and what you want, taking up the cross?

5. *Does this make you happy or sad?*
6. *Does it make Jesus happy?*

Thought Question: Can you think of a time when you helped someone even though it caused you to lose friends?

If somebody is being unkind to one of your friends, what should you do? What does Jesus call this?

CHAPTER 68

Jesus told the people another story. This story was about a man who had two sons. One day the younger son came to his father and said, "Father, give me my share of the estate." He said that he wanted it right away. So his father gave him all the money that he had for him.

The younger son took the money and left his father's house. He went far away to another country. There he wasted and spent all the money his father had given him until it was all gone.

So he had to go to work just to get enough to eat. The man he worked for sent him out to feed the pigs but never gave this young man enough to eat. He got very hungry.

He began to think about his father's house. No one was hungry, not even the people who worked for his father. He had always had plenty to eat there, a bed to sleep in and clean clothes and a father who loved and cared for him. So he said to himself, "I will set out and go back to my father and say to him, 'Father, I have sinned against heaven and against you. I am no longer worthy to be called your son; make me like one of your hired men.' Perhaps he will forgive me and let me work for him."

So he started home, and while he was still far away down the road, his father saw him. His father did not wait for him to come any closer, but ran down the road to meet him. His father was so happy to see him coming home; his father gave him a big hug and kiss.

The son began to tell his father how sorry he was to have been so selfish and greedy to take the money and leave home. But his father was so glad to see him, he wouldn't let him say any more. The father told the people who worked for him to go get new clothes for him to wear and put a ring on his finger and shoes on his feet.

His father also told them to go prepare a big meal, and he told everyone to be happy because his son who had gone away was home again. "I thought he was lost but now he is found," said the father.

Jesus told this story to teach us something. If we have sinned and done something wrong, but are sorry for it and go to our Heavenly Father to tell Him we are sorry, He will always forgive us, just as the father in this story forgave his son.

QUESTIONS—CHAPTER 68

1. *What did the younger son in this story ask his father to give him?*
2. *After he had gone away and spent all the money, what did he have to do to get food to eat?*
3. *Did the man he worked for give him enough to eat?*
4. *What did the son begin to think about?*
5. *What did he do?*
6. *When he was still far down the road, who saw him?*
7. *What did his father do when the son said that he was sorry?*
8. *Will our Heavenly Father forgive us when we tell Him we are sorry when we have sinned?*

Thought Question: Can you imagine how the father felt? Do you think God is happy when we give our hearts to Him? Is sin worth it?

Jesus told the people another story. It was about a rich man who had a lot of money and could buy everything he wanted. He wore beautiful clothes and had good things to eat every day. In the same city where the rich man lived, there was a poor man. His name was Lazarus.

Lazarus was not only poor, but he was sick and weak; his body was covered with sores. Because he was so poor and sick, his friends used to carry him to the rich man's house and lay him down just outside the door, so that he might get the pieces of bread that were left after the rich man was finished eating his dinner.

The dogs that roamed the street seemed to pity Lazarus, for they came and licked his sores.

Finally, poor sick Lazarus died. Then God sent some of His angels to get him.

The angels came and carried Lazarus up to heaven. He was not sick or poor any more when he got to heaven, for God loved him and made him well and gave him everything to make him happy.

After a while the rich man died, too. But the angels did not come for him. He went to the place where wicked men go, called hell. And while he was there, being punished for his sins, he could see Lazarus far away in heaven.

The rich man wanted to go to heaven, where Lazarus was; but he could not, because he had done many bad things and had not asked God to forgive him. Let us ask God to forgive our sins because Jesus paid for them. Let us ask Him to teach us how to love and obey the Lord Jesus. Then, when we die, God will send His angels for us, and they will take us up to heaven, too.

QUESTIONS—CHAPTER 69

1. *What did the rich man in the story have a lot of?*
2. *What was the poor man's name?*
3. *Where did his friends carry him and lay him down?*
4. *When Lazarus died, who came for him and carried him to heaven?*
5. *Was he sick and poor in heaven?*
6. *Where was the rich man sent?*
7. *Why couldn't the rich man go to be with Lazarus in heaven?*
8. *If we ask God to forgive us and ask Jesus to live in our hearts, where will we go when we die?*

Thought Question: Have you ever not helped someone because you thought you were too good?

Parental Note: This chapter deals with the fact of hell. A child can understand this concept because he/she has to deal almost daily with being punished for doing something wrong! But again, you need not dwell on the idea of punishment and hell but instead emphasize heaven and the anticipation of it if we have Jesus in our hearts.

CHAPTER 70

Jesus told a story about two men who went up to the Temple to pray. One of the men thought he was very good, and he wanted other people to think so too. So he stood in a place where other people could see him, and he said his prayers out loud so that the people could hear him. He thought they would believe he was a good man.

But the other man who went up to the Temple to pray did not want other people to hear him. He wanted only God to hear him, for he did not think he was good; he remembered how many times he had sinned, and now he was sorry for it.

So this man went to a place in the Temple where other people would not notice him; and when he prayed, he spoke in a low voice so that no one but God would hear him. This is what he said: "God, have mercy on me, a sinner." Jesus said, "I tell you that this man, rather than the other, went home justified before God. For everyone who exalts himself will be humbled, and he who humbles himself will be exalted." God is not pleased with us when we think we are better than others and when we want other people to praise us and call us good. He is pleased with us when we are sorry for our sins and when we ask Him to forgive us for them.

QUESTIONS—CHAPTER 70

1. *What did the two men in this story go to the Temple to do?*
2. *What did one of them think about himself?*
3. *What did the other man think about himself?*
4. *Which one of the men did Jesus say God was most pleased with?*
5. *Is God pleased with us when we think we are better than other people, and when we want other people to praise us and call us good?*
6. *What should we ask God to forgive us for every day?*

Thought Question: What is the best way to come to Jesus in prayer?

Parental Note: There needs to be a correct balance between our sinfulness and need for forgiveness and God's tender love towards us. Don't make God severe and stern but rather concentrate on His love and what He has done for us through Christ.

Which of these two men did Jesus say God was most pleased with? Which do you think is the proud one?

CHAPTER 71

Some people brought little children to Jesus so that He would touch them and hold them and pray for them. But Jesus' disciples thought this would bother Him, and they told the people to take the children away.

This made Jesus unhappy because He loves little children. He told the disciples, "Let the children come to me and do not hinder them, for the Kingdom of God belongs to such as these." He put the children on His lap, talked to them, and blessed them.

Jesus loves little children. If they will love Him and ask Him to live in their hearts, He will always be with them and take care of them.

QUESTIONS—CHAPTER 71

1. *Who were brought to Jesus?*
2. *Why did the disciples try to send the children away?*
3. *What did Jesus tell the disciples?*
4. *What did Jesus do with the children?*
5. *If children love Jesus and ask Him to live in their hearts, what will He do?*

Thought Question: Why do you think Jesus says that we should be like little children?

Parental Note: See parental note, chapter 13.

These children love Jesus. They've asked Him to live in their hearts. What has Jesus promised to do for these children, and for you, too, if you love Him?

CHAPTER 72

Jesus told the disciples that when He came to the city of Jerusalem, the people who lived there would be very cruel to Him. They would beat Him and would spit upon Him, and after that they would kill Him. They would kill Him by nailing Him to a cross.

A cross was made of two large pieces of wood fastened together. The people would put Jesus on a cross, and they would drive big nails through His hands and His feet into the wood of the cross, so that He could not get away from it. They would leave Him there until He died.

They would do this because they were angry with Him for telling them about their sins and for saying that He was God's Son. The people were very bad. They did not want to be told about their sins, and they would not believe that Jesus was God's Son.

QUESTIONS—CHAPTER 72

1. *How did Jesus say the people would treat Him when He came to Jerusalem?*
2. *What would they nail Him to?*
3. *What was a cross made of?*
4. *Why were the people so angry at Jesus?*
5. *Would they believe that Jesus was God's Son?*

Thought Question: If you had been one of Jesus' disciples and He had told you He was going to be killed, what would you have done?

This is the city of Jerusalem. What did Jesus tell the disciples would happen when He went to the city?

CHAPTER 73

One day Jesus went to a city called Jericho. As He walked down the street, many people followed Him and crowded around Him.

There was a man in Jericho who was blind and very poor. He would sit on the side of the street and beg money from the people who passed him. His name was Bartimaeus.

When Bartimaeus heard the noise of the crowd around Jesus, he asked what was happening. Someone told him that Jesus was passing by. So Bartimaeus yelled out, "Jesus, Son of David, have mercy on me." The people told him to be quiet, but he only yelled louder, "Son of David, have mercy on me."

Jesus heard him and stopped. He told some people to bring Bartimaeus to Him. Bartimaeus was glad when he heard this and hurried to Jesus. Jesus asked Him, "What do you want Me to do for you?" Bartimaeus answered Jesus, "Lord, I want to see."

Jesus said, "Receive your sight." Immediately Bartimaeus could see. He no longer needed people to guide him as he walked down the street. He could do it by himself. And so he followed Jesus.

He thanked God out loud because he had been made well.

QUESTIONS—CHAPTER 73

1. *What was the name of the blind man?*
2. *As soon as Bartimaeus heard that Jesus was passing by, what did he yell out?*
3. *What did Bartimaeus want?*
4. *What did Jesus do?*
5. *How did Jesus make Bartimaeus's eyes well?*
6. *What did Bartimaeus do?*

Thought Question: What are you thankful to God for? Tell someone about it.

Jesus walked down a street like this one when He heard Bartimaeus. What did Bartimaeus call Jesus?

CHAPTER 74

Our government is very large and does many good things for us. But to do those things it needs money, so it taxes us. Each year your mother and daddy pay the government some money out of what they make when they work. That is called a tax.

Long ago, instead of a government taxing people, a king taxed people. And the king would send out men called tax collectors to get the taxes from the people. One of these tax collectors was named Zacchaeus.

When Jesus came to his town, Zacchaeus tried very hard to see Jesus but there was such a big crowd around Him that Zacchaeus could not see Him.

Zacchaeus was a short man and couldn't see over the heads of the other people. So he ran ahead of the crowd and climbed up in a tree and waited there until Jesus passed by under the tree.

When Jesus got to where the tree was, He looked up and saw Zacchaeus and told him, "Zacchaeus, come down immediately. I must stay at your house today." Zacchaeus hurried down from the tree. He was very glad that Jesus was coming to his house.

Zacchaeus listened to all the things Jesus told him, and he promised to do all the things Jesus told him to do. He said, "Look, Lord! Here and now I give half of my possessions to the poor, and if I have cheated anybody out of anything, I will pay back four times that amount."

This made Jesus happy and He told Zacchaeus, "Today salvation has come to this house. . . . For the Son of Man came to seek and to save what was lost."

We must be like Zacchaeus and be kind to other people and help them when we can. We must be very careful never to take anything that belongs to another person. If we have, we must give it back.

This makes Jesus happy.

QUESTIONS—CHAPTER 74

1. *When the government takes money from us, what is that called?*
2. *What was the tax collector's name?*
3. *Why couldn't Zacchaeus see Jesus?*
4. *Where did he go so he could see Jesus?*
5. *When Jesus came to the tree, what did He say to Zacchaeus?*
6. *What did Jesus do for Zacchaeus?*
7. *What can we do to make Jesus happy?*

Thought Question: How would you have felt if you were Zacchaeus and Jesus was coming to your house?

Zacchaeus climbed a tree to see Jesus.

CHAPTER 75

As Jesus was coming to the city of Jerusalem, He told two of His disciples to go into a little town that was nearby. Jesus said they would find a donkey and colt tied there. Jesus told the disciples to untie them and bring them to Him.

If some men should ask why they were taking the animals, the disciples were to say that Jesus had asked for them. Then, Jesus said, the men would let the disciples take them.

So the disciples went to the town and found the donkey and colt tied there, as Jesus had told them they would. As they untied them, some men asked why they did this. The disciples said that Jesus had asked for the donkey and colt. Then the men let the disciples take the donkey and colt, and they brought them to Jesus.

Then Jesus sat on the colt and rode into the city of Jerusalem on the colt's back. A big crowd of people followed after Him as He was riding along. They all cried out, "Blessed is the King Who comes in the name of the Lord. Peace in heaven and glory in the highest." Some of them took off their coats and laid them down on the ground. Other people cut off branches from the trees and laid them on the ground for Jesus to ride over them.

They did this to show how glad they were to have Jesus come into their city. That was what they used to do when a king rode through their streets.

Then Jesus went up to the Temple that was in the city of Jerusalem; and the people brought some people to Him who were blind and others who were lame. Jesus made them well. In the evening He went away from Jerusalem and came to the village named Bethany, which was not far away.

QUESTIONS—CHAPTER 75

1. *What did Jesus send two of His disciples into town to find?*
2. *To what place did Jesus ride on the colt's back?*
3. *What did some of the people put down on the ground for Him to ride over?*
4. *Why did they do this?*
5. *Did the people bring people who were blind and lame to Jesus at the temple?*
6. *What did Jesus do to these persons?*
7. *Where did Jesus go after that?*

Thought Question: Why didn't Jesus take advantage of the people's praise and set Himself up as King?

What were the two animals Jesus told His disciples to fetch from the town nearby? Which one did He ride? What do you think He did with the other animal?

CHAPTER 76

Jesus told the people a story about a man who made a vineyard. A vineyard is a place where grapevines grow. This man planted many grapevines in the ground and made a vineyard.

Then he set up a wall around his vineyard. He built a house there, and he sent some men to stay to take care of his grapevines. But the man himself went away to another country.

After a long while, when it was time for the grapes to be ripe, the man sent someone who worked for him to get some of the grapes to bring to him. But the men who took care of his vineyard would not give any grapes to this man. Then the man sent another person; but the men threw stones at him, and hurt him on the head, and would not give him any grapes either.

Then the man said to himself, What shall I do to make these men obey me? The man had only one son that he loved very much, and he said, "This is what I will do: I will send my only son to them; they will be afraid to hurt him."

So the man sent his son; but when the men saw him coming, they said to one another, "Let us kill him and take the vineyard for our own." As soon as the son came into the vineyard, they grabbed him, and threw him out, and killed him.

Jesus told this story to show what the wicked people in that country were going to do to Him. Jesus was God's Son, and God had sent Him to tell the people they must love and obey Him. But, instead of obeying, they were going to kill His dear Son, just as the wicked men in the vineyard had killed the owner's son.

QUESTIONS—CHAPTER 76

1. *What grows in a vineyard?*
2. *After the man planted his vineyard, what did he put around it?*
3. *What did he do then?*
4. *Whom did he leave to take care of his vineyard?*
5. *What did these men do to the men that the owner sent?*
6. *Whom did he then send to the vineyard?*
7. *What did the men do to his son?*
8. *Why did Jesus tell this story?*
9. *What were the people in that country going to do to Jesus?*

Thought Question: If God knew that Jesus was going to die, why did He let Jesus come to earth?

This is a picture of a large vineyard. Do you know what grows on the green plants?

Jesus told the people another story. It was about a king whose son had just gotten married so the king decided to give a big party. He was going to invite a lot of people to his party. When the party was ready, the king sent his servants out to tell the people that it was time to come. But they would not come.

Then the king sent his servants out again to tell the people that the nice food was on the table waiting for them and that it was time to come to the party. But some of the people would not listen to what the servants told them. Some people listened but did not obey, and others were so mean that they killed the king's servants.

When the king heard what they had done, he was very angry and sent his soldiers out to punish them.

The king then called other servants and told them that although the party was ready, no one was there to eat the food. The people who had been asked to come would not be allowed to come now, since they had refused. It was too late for them.

So the king sent his servants out and found people who would come to the feast. They must go out into the streets and bring everyone they met. The servants brought many people.

But these people did not have clothes that were nice enough to wear to the king's house. So the king had beautiful clothes made for each person. All they had to do was come get them and put them on. As soon as they were dressed, they went into the party and sat down at the table.

When the king came into the room to speak to the people, he saw a man there who did not have on the beautiful new clothes. He asked the man why he came into the feast without them.

But the man was ashamed and could not answer the king. He knew that when those clothes were offered to him, he had not taken them because he was proud and thought his own clothes were good enough.

The king was angry, and he told his servants to take the man out of the party and tie his hands and feet so that he could not get away. They were to take him to the place where he would be punished for not minding the king.

God has given us many good things. He has prepared heaven for us and has given us everything we need in order to enjoy it. All we have to do is to ask Him into our hearts and say thank you.

We must not be like the man who thought his own clothes were good enough even though the king had provided beautiful clothes. Nothing we have or do is good enough to earn us a place in heaven. Asking Jesus into our hearts is the only way to go to heaven.

QUESTIONS—CHAPTER 77

1. *Who made a feast in this story?*
2. *When the king sent his servants to tell the people to come to his feast, what did the people do?*
3. *Did the people who came in from the streets have nice enough clothes to come into the king's house?*
4. *When the king came into the room, did he see there a man without the new clothes?*
5. *Why had this man not put on the new clothes when they were offered to him?*
6. *Did the king tell his servants to take the man away to be punished?*
7. *What do we have to do to go to the wonderful place God has for us?*

Thought Question: Are you good enough to go to heaven on your own?

What does God want us to do more than anything else? Who else does God want us to love besides loving Him? I think these two boys know the answers, don't you?

CHAPTER 78

I told you that the Bible is God's book. It tells us the things that God wants us to do. One day, a man came to Jesus and asked Him what God wanted us to do most. Jesus said, "Love the Lord your God with all your heart, with all your soul, and with all your mind."

We cannot see God, but He is so good to us that we can love Him without seeing Him. Very often people that we love go away where we cannot see them; yet we keep on loving them, and we want to see them.

We will see God when we die, but He wants us to love Him now, before we die. We should love God more than we love anyone else.

And Jesus said there was another thing God wants us to do besides loving Him: He wants us to love each other. If we love each other, we will be kind to each other. God is happy with us when we are kind to each other.

QUESTIONS—CHAPTER 78

1. *Whose book is the Bible?*
2. *What does the Bible tell us?*
3. *What is it that God wants us to do more than anything else?*
4. *Who else does God want us to love beside loving Him?*
5. *If we love one another, how will that make us treat one another?*
6. *Is God happy with us when we are kind to each other?*

Thought Question: What is something you can do this week to be kind to your family?

Jesus wants us to love each other. One way parents love their children is to spend time with them.

CHAPTER 79

Two countries were fighting, and during the fighting a little girl was taken from her home to a place far away. For awhile she missed her home, but she loved God and trusted Him. Soon she learned to love the new people and her new home. The people where she lived did not know or love God.

This little girl worked for a nice lady whose husband, Naaman, was an important soldier in the king's army. But Naaman was very sick. He had leprosy. Remember I told you what leprosy was? The little girl was sad that he was so sick and told his wife that back in her old home, there was a prophet, Elisha, who could cure his leprosy.

Naaman went to the king to ask if he could go to this other country, and the king said yes. Naaman's king wrote a letter to the king of the other country asking him to cure Naaman. This new king was very upset because he knew he could not cure Naaman's leprosy. Elisha heard that the king was upset and sent a message telling the king to send Naaman to him.

So Naaman went to Elisha's house, but Elisha didn't come out to meet him. He sent out a messenger, who told him, "Go wash yourself seven times in the Jordan, and your flesh will be restored and you will be cleansed." Naaman got angry. He thought that Elisha was rude not to come out to talk to him. And he didn't want to go wash in the Jordan River—it was very muddy. So he decided to go back home instead of doing what Elisha said.

On their way back home, a man who worked for Naaman came to him and asked, "If the prophet had told you to do some great thing would you not have done it? How much more reason, then, to obey him when he tells you, 'wash and be cleansed.'" Naaman realized that this man was right, so he turned to go to the Jordan River.

When he got to the river, it was just as muddy as ever. But he went in and washed once. Nothing happened. Twice, three times—even after he had washed six times—nothing had happened. But when he washed the seventh time he came out with no leprosy. He was completely well, just as Elisha had said. Naaman was very happy.

Naaman went back to Elisha's house to thank him. This time Elisha met him at the door. Naaman told Elisha that now he believed in God.

Naaman began to love God because that one little girl, even though she was far from home, still loved and obeyed God.

It took a lot of courage for her to tell Naaman's wife about Elisha and her God, but she trusted God and was not afraid to talk about Him to others.

QUESTIONS—CHAPTER 79

1. What disease did Naaman have?
2. Who told him to go see Elisha?
3. Could the king cure Naaman?
4. What did Elisha tell Naaman to do?
5. Did he obey right away?
6. Was he well after washing five times?
7. How many times did he have to wash?
8. Why did Naaman go back to Elisha's house?
9. What did he tell Elisha?
10. Why did the little girl tell Naaman about Elisha?

Thought Question: Why do you think Naaman was mad that Elisha didn't come to the door the first time and that he was told to go wash in the Jordan?

Parental Note: It is important for children to learn early to talk about Jesus with others. Witnessing is such an important key to our growth as Christians, and children who grow up doing it with ease and naturalness will have a more vital faith.

CHAPTER 80

There were some men in Jesus' country called Pharisees. These men used to say their prayers out in the open, where people could hear them. They wanted the people to think that they were good, and they wanted praise from other people. And whenever anyone was looking at them, they were very careful to do what was right; but when no one saw them, they did what was wrong.

Jesus said we shouldn't be like the Pharisees. We should not say our prayers for other people to hear, but for God to hear us. We shouldn't do right because we want other people to think we are good, but because God tells us to do right, and because we want to please Him.

QUESTIONS—CHAPTER 80

1. *Where did the men called Pharisees say their prayers?*
2. *Why did they want the people to hear them?*
3. *When anybody was looking at them, what were the Pharisees very careful to do?*
4. *But when no one saw them, what did they do?*
5. *Should we be like the Pharisees?*
6. *Who do we want to hear our prayers?*
7. *Who sees us all the time?*
8. *Should we do the right thing because we want to please Him?*

Thought Question: Is it easier to be good when someone is watching you?

I hope you say your prayers each night at bedtime. Is that the only time you should pray?

CHAPTER 81

I told you before about the beautiful church called the Temple. Some ministers always stayed at the Temple, and the people who went there used to give them money. The people did not put money into the ministers' hands, but dropped it into a box that had a hole in the top.

Every person dropped in just as much as he wanted to. After a lot had been dropped in, the ministers opened the box and took the money out. They bought things with it for the Temple. This money was the same as if it were given to God; it was God's money.

One day Jesus saw the people who came to drop their money into the box. Some of them who were rich dropped in a lot. After a while, a poor woman who was a widow (that means her husband was dead) came and dropped in only a little bit of money.

Then Jesus called His disciples to Him, and told them, "I tell you the truth, this poor widow has put in more than all the others. All these people gave their gifts out of their wealth; but she out of her poverty put in all she had to live on."

The rich people had plenty of money left over for themselves. But the poor woman had nothing left for herself, because she gave all that she had and did not save enough even to buy herself bread. This showed how much she loved God. God wants us to love Him more than He wants us to do anything else.

QUESTIONS—CHAPTER 81

1. *What did the people give to the ministers who stayed at the Temple?*
2. *Who gave the large amount of money?*
3. *Who came and dropped in a little bit of money?*
4. *Which did God think the most of?*
5. *Did the poor woman have any left for herself?*
6. *Did she give all she had to God?*
7. *What did this show?*
8. *What does God want us to do more than anything else?*

Thought Question: What do you have that you can give to Jesus?

Parental Note: Tithing is an important concept in our Christian faith. It should be taught early and made a life-long habit—to give back to God a portion of that which He has so bountifully given to us. Help your child to see that it is a joy to give to God and we do it because we love Him.

When you go to Sunday school and church, I'm sure you always remember to take your offering. God gives us so many gifts, it's fun for us to give something back to Him.

Jesus told a story about some young women who went out in the night, carrying lamps with them. They went out to meet a man who had just been married. This man was called the bridegroom, and now the bridegroom was coming home to his house.

These young women went out to meet him. Because the bridegroom stayed longer than they expected, they sat down to wait until he should come. And they all fell asleep.

In the middle of the night somebody woke them up and said, "The bridegroom is coming; go out to meet him." They all got up quickly and began to get ready. But they found that while they were asleep their lamps had gone out because all the oil had been used up.

Now, some of the young women were wise and had brought extra oil with them; now they poured this oil into their lamps and lighted them again. Then they were ready when the bridegroom came, and he took them with him into his house and gave them a feast.

But the other women were foolish; they did not bring any extra oil with them, so they had to go away to buy some. By the time they came back, it was too late; the bridegroom had gone into his house and shut the door. They could not get in.

This is the way it will be when Jesus comes again. Some people will be ready like the wise young women who had their lamps burning. And Jesus will take those who are ready up to heaven. So Jesus said, "Therefore, keep watch, because you do not know the day or the hour."

But some people, like the foolish young women whose lamps were out when the bridegroom came, will not be ready and they cannot go with Jesus up to heaven. If we want to be ready for Jesus when He comes back, we must love Him and ask Him to be our Savior.

QUESTIONS—CHAPTER 82

1. *What did the young women who went out at night carry in their hands?*
2. *Whom did they go out to meet?*
3. *When they woke up, what had happened to their lamps?*
4. *Why had the lamps gone out?*
5. *What had the wise young women brought with them?*
6. *And were they ready when the bridegroom came?*
7. *Did the bridegroom take them with him into his feast?*
8. *Had the foolish young women brought any more oil?*
9. *What did they have to do to get some?*
10. *When they came back, could they go into the feast?*
11. *Where will Jesus take the people who are ready to meet Him when He comes?*
12. *If we want to be ready to meet Jesus when He comes, what must we do?*

Thought Question: What would happen if Jesus came today?

Parental Note: This chapter introduces the Second Coming of Christ. This is the exciting hope of our faith, and your excitement will be contagious!

CHAPTER 83

Jesus told the disciples about when He was going to come back to earth again. That is called the Second Coming. The Second Coming will happen in the last days in history. Jesus will come from heaven on that day, and all the angels will come with Him. Then He will sit on a throne, where everyone can see Him.

You and I will see Him. The people who are dead and buried in their graves will come to life again at the Second Coming. Jesus will call them, and they will hear Him and will come up out of their graves. They, too, will see Jesus.

The people who have loved Jesus and obeyed Him will stand on one side, and the people who have not obeyed Him will stand on the other side. Then Jesus will take all those who have loved Him to heaven to live with Him forever, but those who have not loved Him will be sent away from Him forever.

QUESTIONS—CHAPTER 83

1. *What will happen in the last days in history?*
2. *Who is coming to this world at the Second Coming?*
3. *Who will come with Jesus?*
4. *Where will He sit?*
5. *Will you and I see Him?*
6. *What will happen to all the people who are dead?*
7. *Where will Jesus take the good people who have loved Him?*
8. *What will happen to the people who have not loved Jesus?*

Thought Question: What would it be like to be sent away from Jesus forever?

Long ago, people thought heaven was up in the sky. We don't know where heaven is, but we do know that Jesus will return one day to take us there, if we love Him.

CHAPTER 84

Do you remember that I told you that the disciples were the men who stayed with Jesus all the time? They followed Him wherever He went and listened to what He taught them. There were twelve disciples and all of them loved Jesus—all except one. This one disciple, named Judas, loved money more than anything else. He did not love Jesus.

Judas went to the men who wanted to kill Jesus and asked them how much money they would give him if he showed them where Jesus was. The men told him that if he would show them where Jesus was so that they could go and take Him, they would give Judas thirty pieces of silver.

Judas decided that as soon as he could find Jesus in a place by Himself, he would show these wicked men where Jesus was. Then they could get Jesus and take Him away to kill Him.

QUESTIONS—CHAPTER 84

1. *How many disciples were there?*
2. *Did they all love Jesus?*
3. *Which one didn't love Jesus?*
4. *What did Judas love more than anything else?*
5. *What did Judas ask the men who wanted to kill Jesus?*
6. *How much money did they promise to give him?*
7. *What did Judas decide to do?*

This money is like the money Judas was given. These are Roman coins that were used in Jesus' day.

MEMORY VERSE—Titus 2:13 . . . We wait for the blessed hope—the glorious appearing of our great God and Savior, Jesus Christ.

The people who lived in Jesus' country used to have a feast. A feast is a meal that is eaten for a special reason. They had this feast once a year; in fact, Jewish people still have this feast. It is called the feast of the Passover.

It was now time for Jesus and His disciples to eat the feast of the Passover, and they wanted to do it together. But they did not have a place in which to eat, so the disciples asked Jesus where they should go to get the feast ready. Jesus told them to go into town and as they got there they would see a man carrying a pitcher of water. When they saw this man, they were to follow him into a house and tell him that Jesus had sent them and ask him to show them where they could feast.

The disciples did exactly what Jesus told them to do, and the man carrying the pitcher showed them a room for them to use. It had a long table and seats around the table. So the disciples got the feast ready.

That evening, about suppertime, Jesus came and sat down at the table. He told the disciples this would be the last time that He would eat the Passover feast with them. Very soon, He said, He would be taken away. He said this because He knew that He would die soon because the people were going to kill Him.

Then Jesus told the disciples that He was going to heaven to make a place ready for them and that later He would come back to take them to Heaven. Jesus meant that He would come back and get all those people who love Him when He comes at the Second Coming.

After they had eaten, they sang a song together and left. Then they went to a garden. Jesus went off by Himself in the garden to kneel down and pray.

Jesus knew that some men were going to come and take Him that night and kill Him. He told God, His Father, "My Father, if it is possible, may this cup be taken from Me. Yet not as I will, but as You will." He didn't want to die, but He knew that it was the only way that we could have our sins forgiven and go to heaven.

QUESTIONS—CHAPTER 85

1. *What was the name of the feast that was celebrated by Jesus and His disciples?*
2. *What were the disciples to ask the man*

who lived in the house to show them?
3. *Did the disciples obey Jesus?*
4. *What did Jesus tell the disciples while they were eating?*
5. *What did Jesus know that the people were going to do to Him?*
6. *Where did He say He was going to make a place ready for them?*
7. *Is Jesus going to come back and take all those who love Him to heaven?*

8. *After the feast where did Jesus and the disciples go?*
9. *What did Jesus do in the garden?*
10. *Why was Jesus willing to die?*

Thought Question: What kind of place do you think heaven will be?

Parental Note: Here is a small bit of cultural background. You may want to study up on the Jewish feasts and celebrations.

Jesus and his disciples are eating a meal. What is this meal called? What is Jesus telling the disciples?

CHAPTER 86

Judas, the wicked disciple, did not go into the garden with Jesus, but he was watching to see where Jesus went. When Judas saw that Jesus had gone to the garden, he thought it would be a good time for him to go and tell the men who wanted to kill Jesus.

So Judas went to those men and told them where Jesus had gone. The men gave Judas the thirty pieces of silver they had promised him.

They sent some men with Judas to go get Jesus. These men carried sticks and swords to fight with. They carried lanterns, too, so that they could see in the dark, because it was nighttime. Judas went with the men to show them the way to the garden.

While they were going, he told them how they would know which one was Jesus. Judas said that as soon as they came into the garden, he would go up to Jesus and kiss Him, and then, he said, the men should take Jesus and hold Him tightly.

So Judas went with the men to the garden. He went up to Jesus, and pretended he was glad to see Him. He said, "Greetings, Rabbi," and kissed Him. As soon as he had kissed Him, the men grabbed Jesus and took Him away.

QUESTIONS—CHAPTER 86

1. *Did Judas go with Jesus into the garden?*
2. *When he found that Jesus had gone there, who did he go and tell?*
3. *What did those men give Judas?*
4. *How did Judas say they would know which one was Jesus?*
5. *After Judas had kissed Jesus, what did the men do to Him?*

Thought Question: How do you think Jesus felt when Judas kissed him and then let the men take him away?

Jesus and His disciples went to this garden after their meal. Who came to the garden looking for Jesus?

When the disciples saw the men taking Jesus, they were angry and were going to fight with them. One of the disciples, named Peter, took a sword and hit one of the men with it and cut off his ear. But Jesus told Peter, "Put your sword back in its place." Then Jesus touched the man's ear, and made it well again.

Jesus did not want the disciples to fight for Him. He said that God would send down many angels from heaven to fight for Him if He asked for them. But Jesus would not ask for them. He was willing to let the men take Him, and He was willing to let them kill Him.

Why was Jesus willing to let the men kill Him? Because that was the way He was going to be punished in our place for all the sins that we have done.

So the men took Jesus with them out of the garden. Then the disciples were afraid that the men would take them too, and they ran away and left Jesus alone with the men.

QUESTIONS—CHAPTER 87

1. *How did the disciples feel when they saw the men taking Jesus away?*
2. *What did the disciple named Peter do?*
3. *What did Jesus do to the man's ear?*
4. *Did He want the disciples to fight for Him?*
5. *Why was Jesus willing to let the men kill Him?*
6. *When the disciples saw the men taking Jesus away, what did they do?*
7. *What would you have done?*

These men are acting out what happened in the garden. Who is the man holding a sword? What did he do with it? What did Jesus say?

CHAPTER 88

In our country, when a man has done wrong, he is brought before a judge who tells him what his punishment will be. But in Jesus' day, the governor was the one who punished the people for doing wrong. The men who wanted to kill Jesus took Him to the governor and told the governor that Jesus had done wrong and should be punished.

These men were very bad because they lied when they said Jesus had done wrong. Jesus had not done wrong. These men said that Jesus was bad and should be killed.

The governor was a cruel man. He had his soldiers beat Jesus with a whip. It hurt Jesus and cut His skin. They got some thorny branches and wound them together and pushed them down on Jesus' head. They spit on Him and called Him names.

After that the soldiers got a cross made of wood and stretched Jesus out on it. They hammered great big nails through His hands and feet to fasten Him to the cross.

It hurt Jesus very much, but He did all of that for you and me. He loves us that much.

The soldiers then stood the cross up with Jesus nailed to it, and they stayed there to watch Him die.

QUESTIONS—CHAPTER 88

1. *What did the men who wanted to kill Jesus tell the governor about Him?*
2. *Were they lying?*
3. *What did the governor do?*
4. *What did the soldiers do?*
5. *What did the soldiers nail Him to?*
6. *Why did Jesus go through all of that?*

This picture shows what Jesus might have looked like on the cross. Do you know why Jesus allowed Himself to be killed?

CHAPTER 89

Mark 15:42–47; 16:1–7; Matthew 28:1–10

There was a rich man named Joseph who loved Jesus. When Joseph saw that Jesus was dead, he went to the governor and asked him to let him take Jesus down from the cross and bury Him. The governor said okay.

So Joseph came to the place where they had killed Jesus, and he pulled out the big nails that they had nailed through His hands and His feet; and he took Jesus down from the cross.

Joseph wrapped up Jesus' dead body in some new, clean cloth that he had bought. A good man named Nicodemus helped Joseph. They buried Jesus in a tomb that was hollowed out of a rock. Some women who loved Jesus came and saw where they buried Him. The men rolled a big stone in front of the tomb to close it up. They went away and left Jesus there.

Then the governor sent some soldiers to watch the tomb, and to keep Jesus' disciples away.

But early in the morning, while it was still dark, God sent an angel from heaven. The angel's face was bright, like lightning, and his clothes were as white as snow. When the soldiers saw the angel, they were afraid, and they trembled and fell down on the ground. They could not move. They were like dead men.

Some women had come to look at the tomb of Jesus, and they were wondering who would roll away the big stone for them. But when they got there, the stone was already rolled away, and an angel was beside it. The women were afraid. But the angel said, "Do not be afraid, for I know that you are looking for Jesus, who was crucified. He is not here; He has risen."

You remember how He had told His disciples before that the people would kill Him and bury Him in the grave. And He had told them also that He would come to life again and would come out of the grave after He had been buried. Now Jesus did what He had said by coming to life again and coming out of the grave.

QUESTIONS—CHAPTER 89

1. *Who asked the governor to let him bury Jesus?*
2. *Who came to help Joseph?*
3. *Where did they bury Jesus?*
4. *What did they roll over the door of the tomb?*
5. *Whom did the governor send to watch over the tomb?*

6. *Whom did God send in the early morning?*
7. *What happened to the soldiers when they saw the angel?*
8. *What did the women see when they arrived?*
9. *What did the angel tell them?*
10. *Had Jesus told the apostles, before, that He would come to life again?*

Thought Question: Can you imagine how you would have felt if you had been at the tomb of Jesus that Easter morning?

Here is a tomb like the one where Joseph buried Jesus. Can you see the big round stone which is used to close the doorway?

CHAPTER 90

After He came out of the grave, Jesus went to the disciples. They were in a room together, with the door of the room closed, but Jesus came into the room. When the disciples saw Him, they were afraid. They didn't think it was Jesus; they thought He was dead.

But Jesus told them not to be afraid. Then He showed them His hands and His feet with the scars from the nails in them, so they might know that it was Jesus and that He had really come to life again.

Jesus told the disciples, "Therefore go and make disciples of all nations, baptizing them in the name of the Father and of the Son and of the Holy Spirit, and teaching them to obey everything I have commanded you." He wanted everyone to know how much He loved them and that He had been punished in their place by dying on the cross for them. The disciples were not only to tell the people who lived in that country about it, but they were to go all over the world to tell every person.

Jesus wanted you and me to be told about it, too, so that we might know how much He loved us and so that we might love Him and be willing to do everything that He tells us to do.

QUESTIONS—CHAPTER 90

1. *After He had come out of the grave, with whom did Jesus go and talk?*
2. *How did the disciples feel when they saw Jesus?*
3. *Why were they afraid?*
4. *What did Jesus show them so they might know He had really come to life again?*
5. *What did He tell the disciples to do?*
6. *Did He want you and me to be told about this too?*
7. *Why did He want us to be told about it?*

Thought Question: Do you know some people who live far away in order to tell the people there about Jesus? They are called missionaries. How can you be a missionary?

In this seventeenth-century painting, Jesus showed His disciples the scars on His hands and the wound in His side. Can you see them?

CHAPTER 91

After Jesus had talked with the disciples, He took them out of the city to a place by themselves. While He was speaking to them there, all at once He began to go up from them toward the sky. He went up higher and higher, until they saw Him go into a cloud; and they could not see Him any more.

Then two angels came and told the disciples, "Men of Galilee, why do you stand here looking into the sky? This same Jesus, Who has been taken from you into heaven, will come back in the same way you have seen Him go into heaven." Jesus is in heaven now. But He sees all the little children who love Him and mind Him. He hears them when they pray to Him, and He helps them to be good.

They don't ever need be afraid, for He does not forget them, but He loves them and will take care of them. And when He comes to this world again, at the Second Coming, He will call them all to Him; and He will take them to heaven, and they will stay with Him there always.

QUESTIONS—CHAPTER 91

1. *While Jesus was speaking to the disciples, where did He begin to go?*
2. *Could they see Him any more after that?*
3. *Who came then and spoke to the disciples?*
4. *Where did the angels say that Jesus had gone?*
5. *Where is He now?*
6. *Does He see all the little children who love Him and mind Him?*
7. *Does He ever forget them?*
8. *Does He love them and take care of them?*
9. *Where will He take them when He comes again at the Second Coming?*
10. *How long will they stay with Jesus in heaven?*

When you look up at the beautiful sky, why don't you tell Jesus that you love Him? Ask Him to come into your heart and take care of you. He has promised that He will and that He will come back one day to take us to live with Him forever.